EDUCATIONAL SPACES

A PICTORIAL REVIEW OF SIGNIFICANT SPACES

VOLUME 1

EDUCATIONAL SPACES

VOLUME 1

A PICTORIAL REVIEW OF SIGNIFICANT SPACES

ISBN 1 86470 013 0
© 1998
The Images Publishing Group Pty Ltd
Melbourne, Australia 1998
Printed in Singapore

CONTENTS

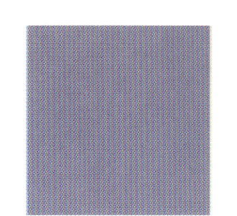

Primary and Secondary Spaces   **7**

Adult Spaces   **57**

Designers' Biographies   213

Index   221

Acknowledgments   224

"A jug fills drop by drop"
— Gautama Buddha

Primary and Secondary Education Spaces

Aichi Children's Center
Nagakute, Nagoya, Japan
Mitsuru Senda & Environment Design Institute
1 Main floor plan
2 Children's elevator
3 Handicraft studio
4 Atrium
5&6 Skybridge
7 Challenge tower and skybridge
Photo credit: Mitsumasa Fujitsuka

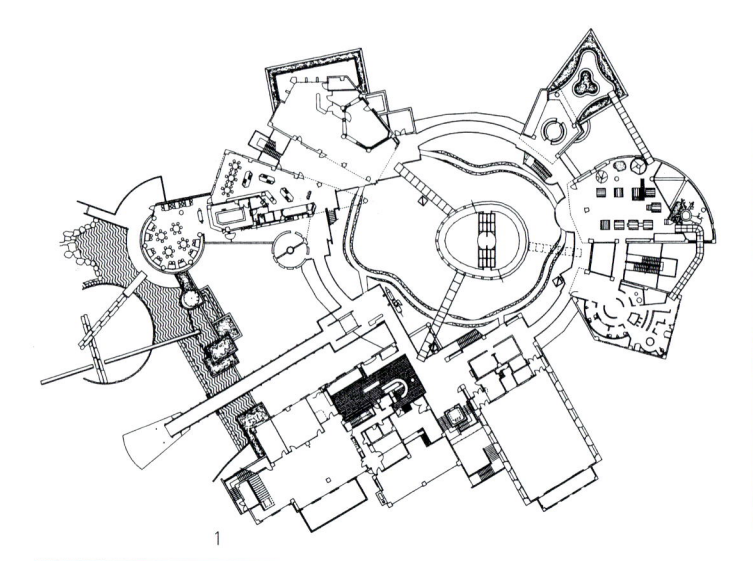

Primary and Secondary Education **9**

**Leonardo Centre at Uppingham School
Rutland, UK**
CZWG Architects
1 Parapeted eastern entrance front facing the new quadrangle
2 Ground floor plan
3 Cascade of patent glazing at north elevation
4 North lit artroom with light fittings formation after Magritte

Photo credit: Andrew Putler

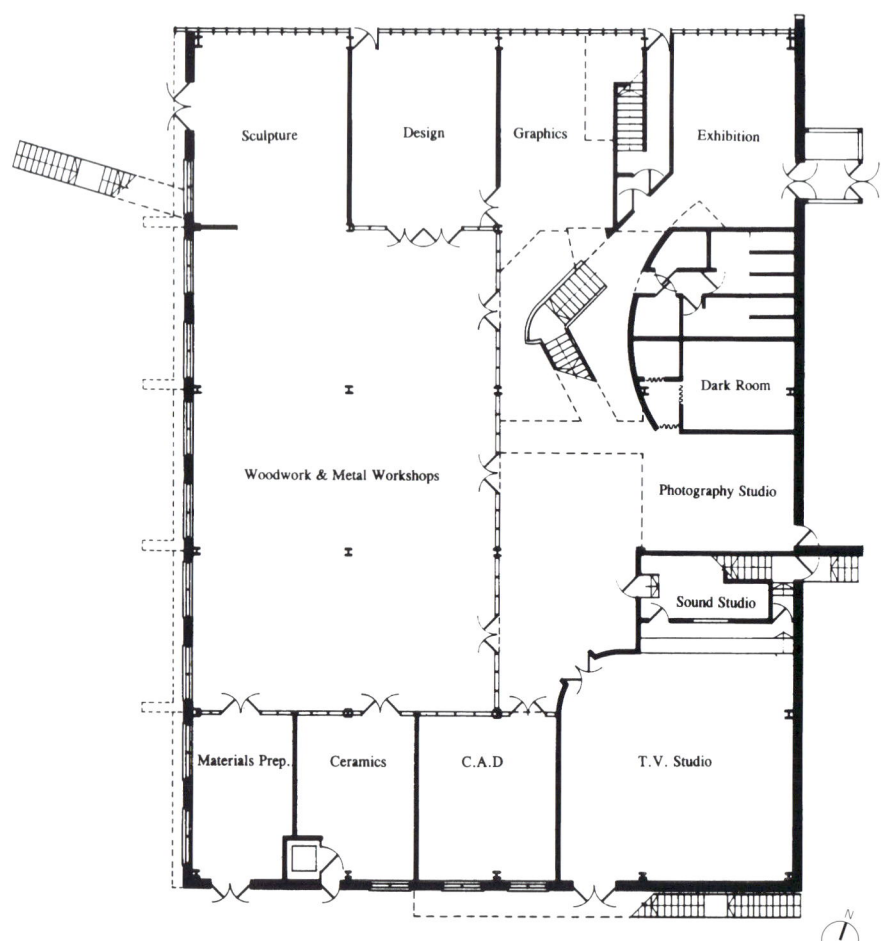

Primary and Secondary Education **11**

**Leonardo Centre at Uppingham School
Rutland, UK**
CZWG Architects

5   Central well in brilliantly north lit art area
Opposite:
    Central composition of red sail, twisting
    stair and blue staff room
Photo credit: Andrew Putler

UPPINGHAM

Fairley House School
Pimlico, London, UK
Jestico + Whiles

1 External view of building
2 Porthole window detail
3 Secure stairwell

Photo credit: Paul Rattigan
courtesy Jestico + Whiles

Bousfield School Nursery
South Kensington, London, UK
Austin-Smith:Lord

4 View across entrance forecourt
5 Playroom classroom

Photo credit: Alan Williams

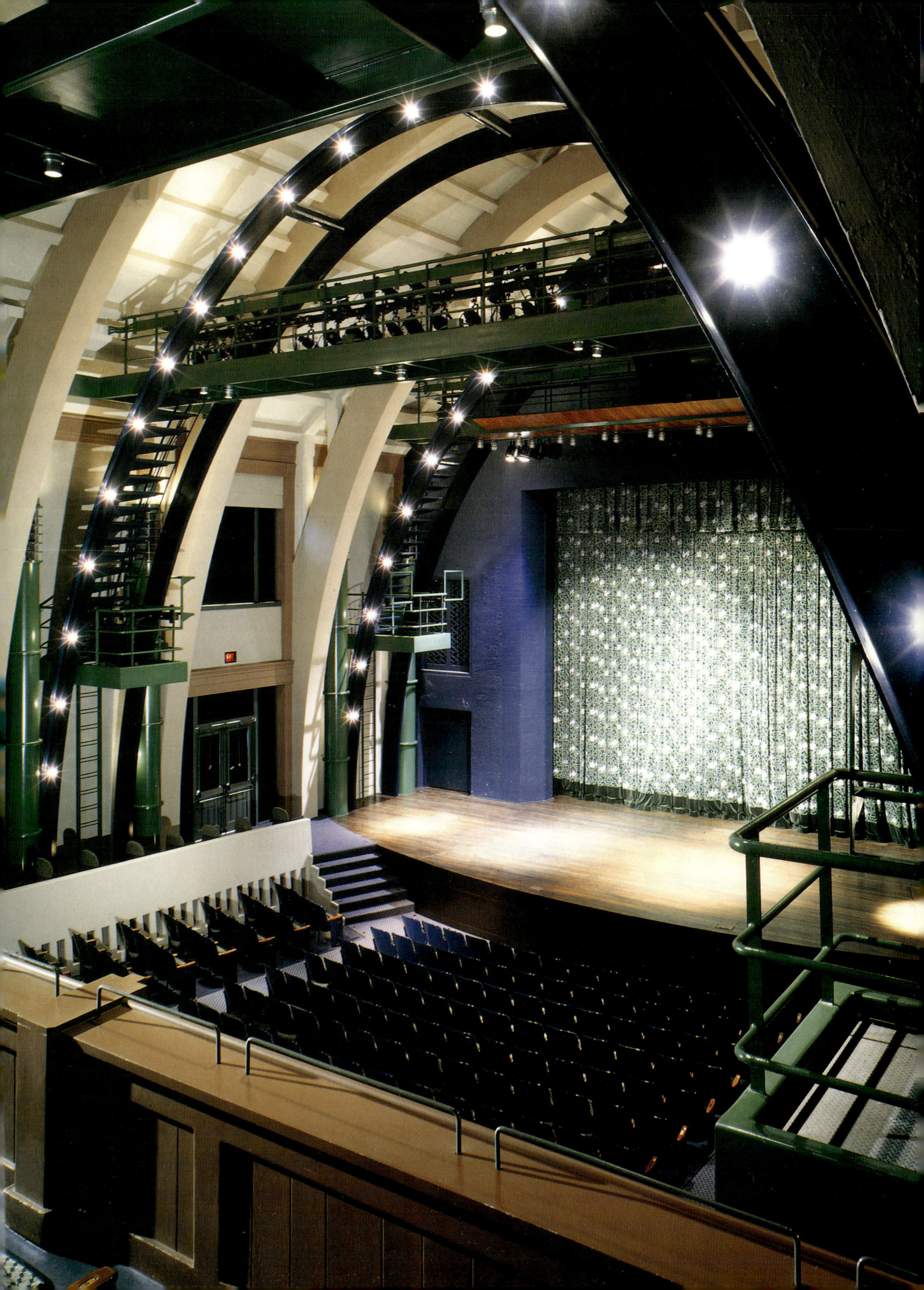

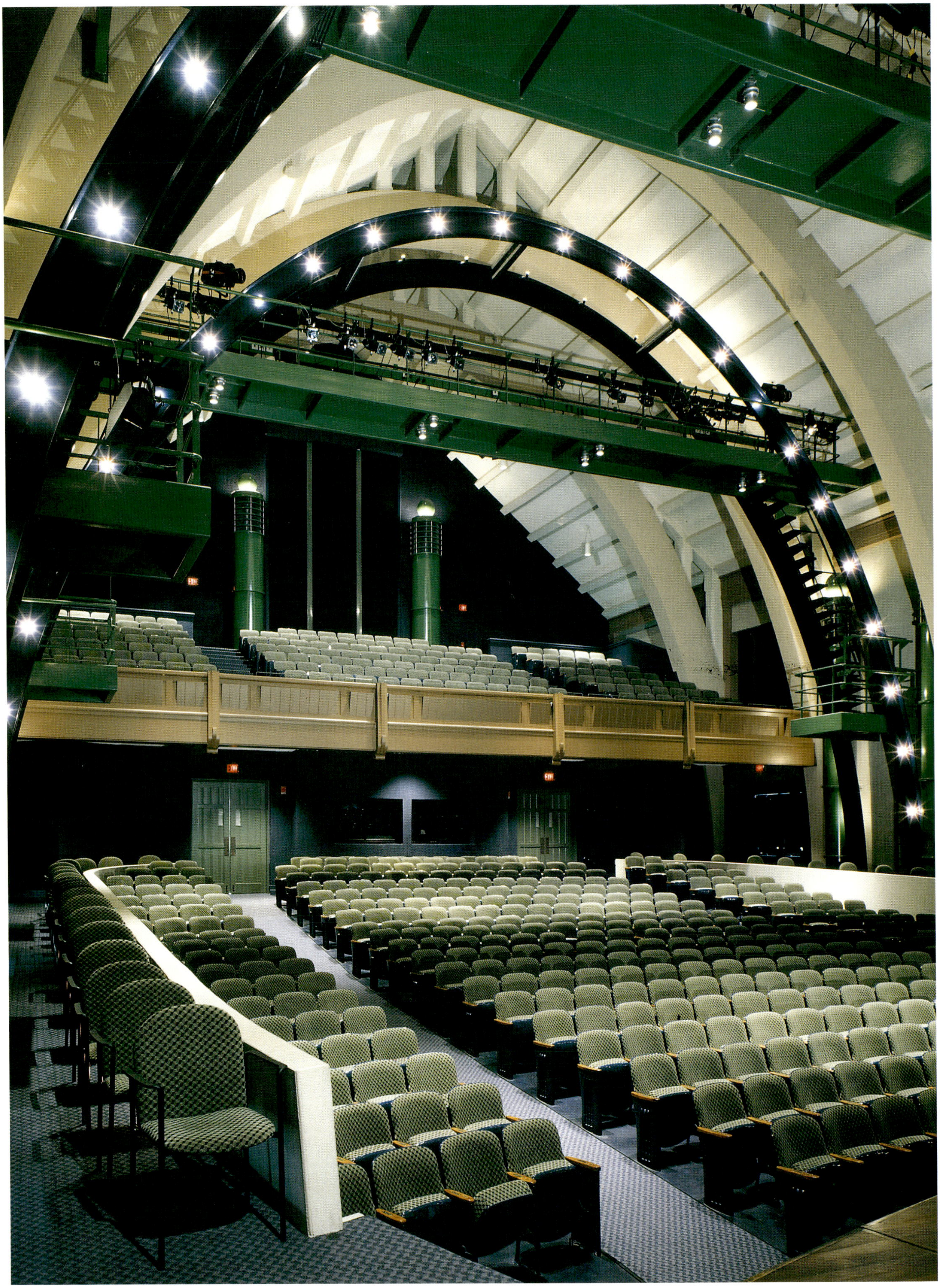

9

10

11

**Dillingham Hall, Punahou School
Honolulu, Hawaii, USA**
Hardy Holzman Pfeiffer Associates
Previous page:
 View towards stage
8 View of the auditorium as seen from stage
9 View of exterior showing entrance facade
Photo credit: David Franzen

**St. Michael's Primary School
Singapore**
Alfred Wong Partnership Pty Ltd
10 View from entrance to school
11 Canopy covered walkways linking the classrooms
12 The concourse
Photo credit: courtesy Alfred Wong Partnership Pty Ltd

12

Primary and Secondary Education 17

Rumsey Hall School
Washington Depot, Connecticut, USA
The S/L/A/M Collaborative
1 New lower school quadrangle
2 John Seward Johnson, Sr. Fine Arts Center
3 Lower school building
4 Kindergarten classroom
5 Typical lower school classroom
Photo credit: Woodruff/Brown Photography

Primary and Secondary Education **19**

**Mary Tisko and Mary Murphy Schools
Branford, Connecticut, USA**
Roth and Moore Architects

1 Axonometric
2 Fenestration in stairway provides natural light at end of corridor
3 Built-in window seat within classroom bay window
4 The new library, lunchroom and entry pavilions are visually connected by bus loading covered arcade
5 Scissor trusses of laminated timber frame refectory form of lunchroom and library pavilions

Photo credit: Steve Rosenthal

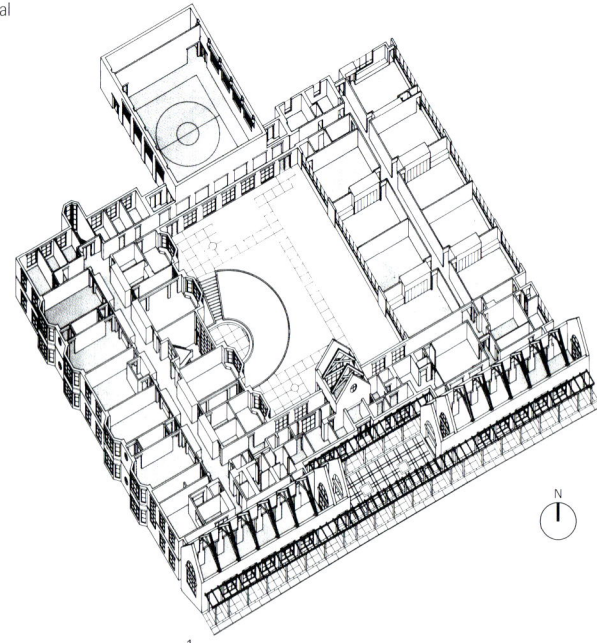

Primary and Secondary Education 21

1
2
3
4

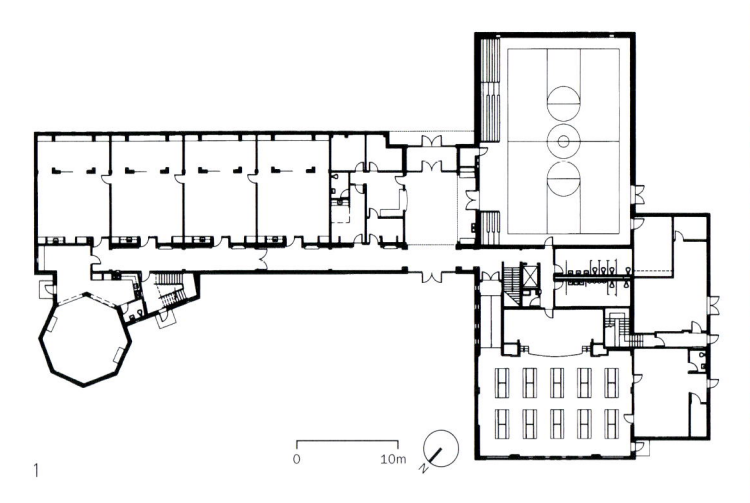

Royalston Community School
Royalston, Massachusetts, USA
TAMS Consultants, Inc.

1 First floor plan
2 Entry approach to school
3 Octagonal classroom tower overlooking meadow and woods
4 Entry lobby, second floor bridge
5 Single loaded corridor animated with random window openings and floor pattern
6 Library reading room overlooking the woods

Photo credit: Chuck Choi

Primary and Secondary Education

Connecticut Junior Republic
Litchfield, Connecticut, USA
The S/L/A/M Collaborative

1 Multi-purpose room and student courtyard
2 Classroom wing as seen from road
3 Library and multi-purpose room bordering student courtyard
4 Multi-purpose room
5 Library/media centre

Photo credit: Woodruff/Brown Photography

Primary and Secondary Education 25

**Ishibashi Junior High School
Japan**
Kisho Kurokawa Architect & Associates
1 First floor plan
2 General view
3 West elevation
4 Corridor
5 Atrium
Photo credit: Tomio Ohashi

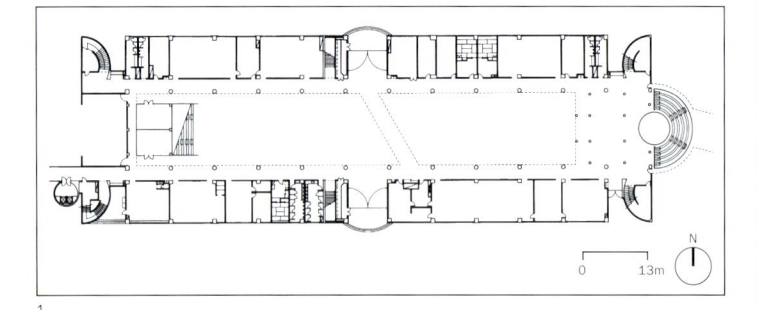

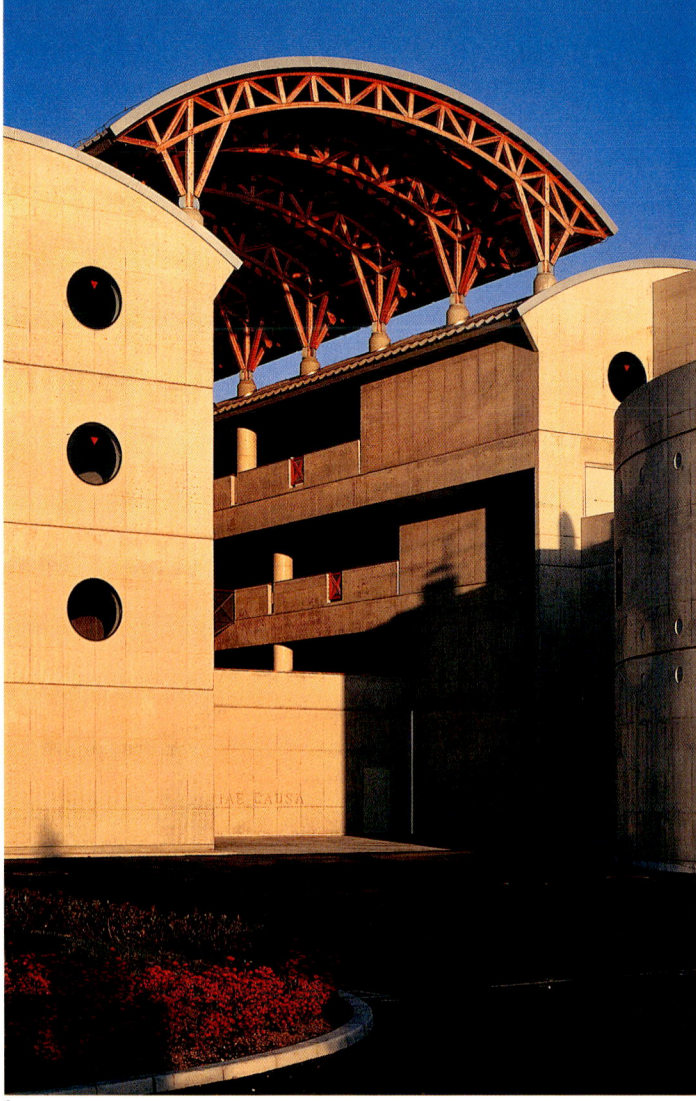

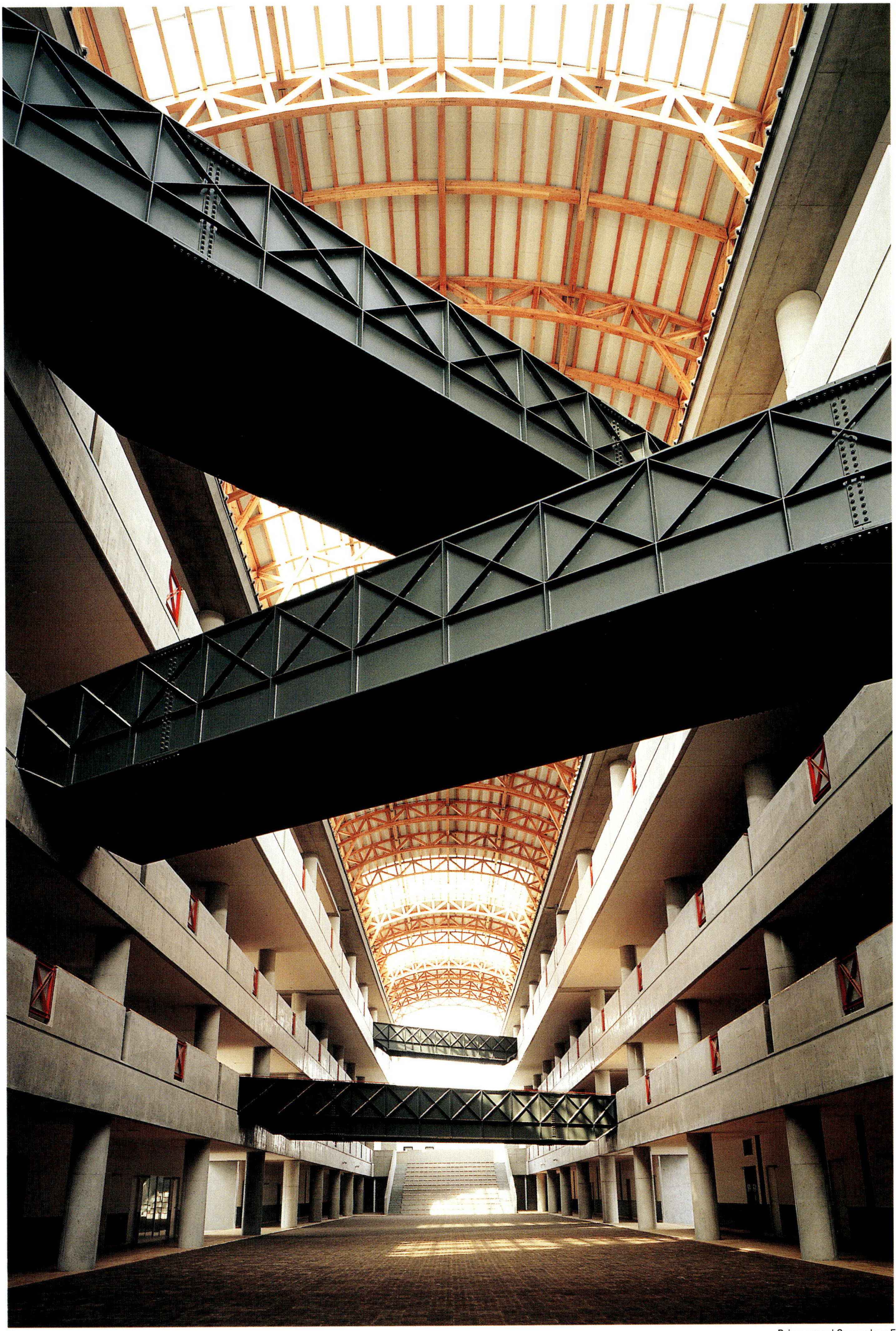

5

6

7

Ishibashi Junior High School
Japan
Kisho Kurokawa Architect & Associates
6 Corridor
7 Classroom
8 Indoor sports area, west view
9 Indoor sports area, southeast elevation
10 Gymnasium
Photo credit: Tomio Ohashi

Misumi Public Elementary School
Mishumi-cho, Naka-gun, Shimane Pref., Japan
Shin Takamatsu Architects & Associates

1 Overall view
2 Ground floor plan
3 Staircase, a concrete box facing the pond contains library and music room
4 Night view, pond surrounded by corridor
5 Overall view, showing gymnasium on right hand side
6 View to the patio through corridor
7 Open space

Photo credit: Mr Toshiyuki Kobayashi

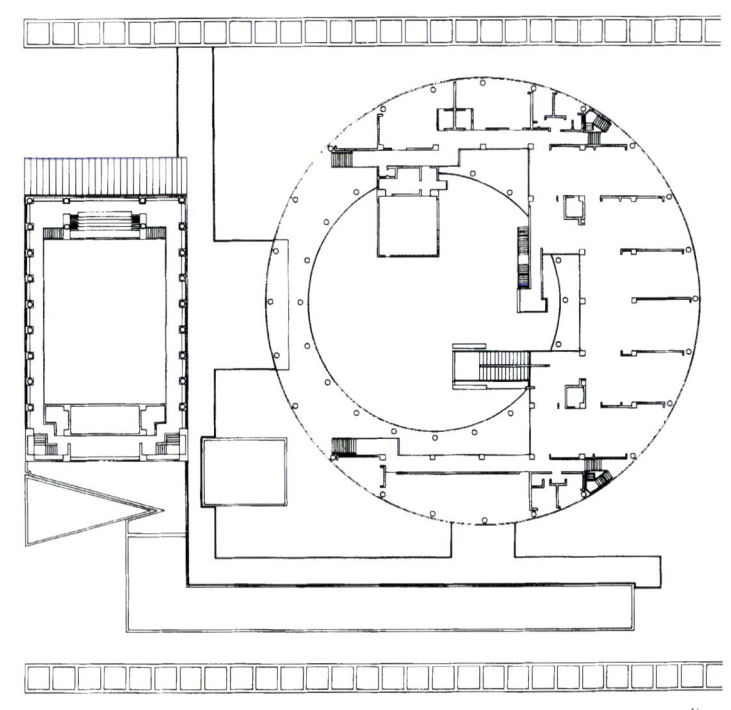

Primary and Secondary Education

City View Elementary School
Worcester, Massachusetts, USA
TAMS Consultants, Inc.
1 First level floor plan
2 Cafeteria exterior, glazed wall between solid masses
3 Cafeteria interior wall of light
4 School entrance facade
5 Detail of exhaust stacks and curved wall of cafeteria

Photo credit: Chuck Choi

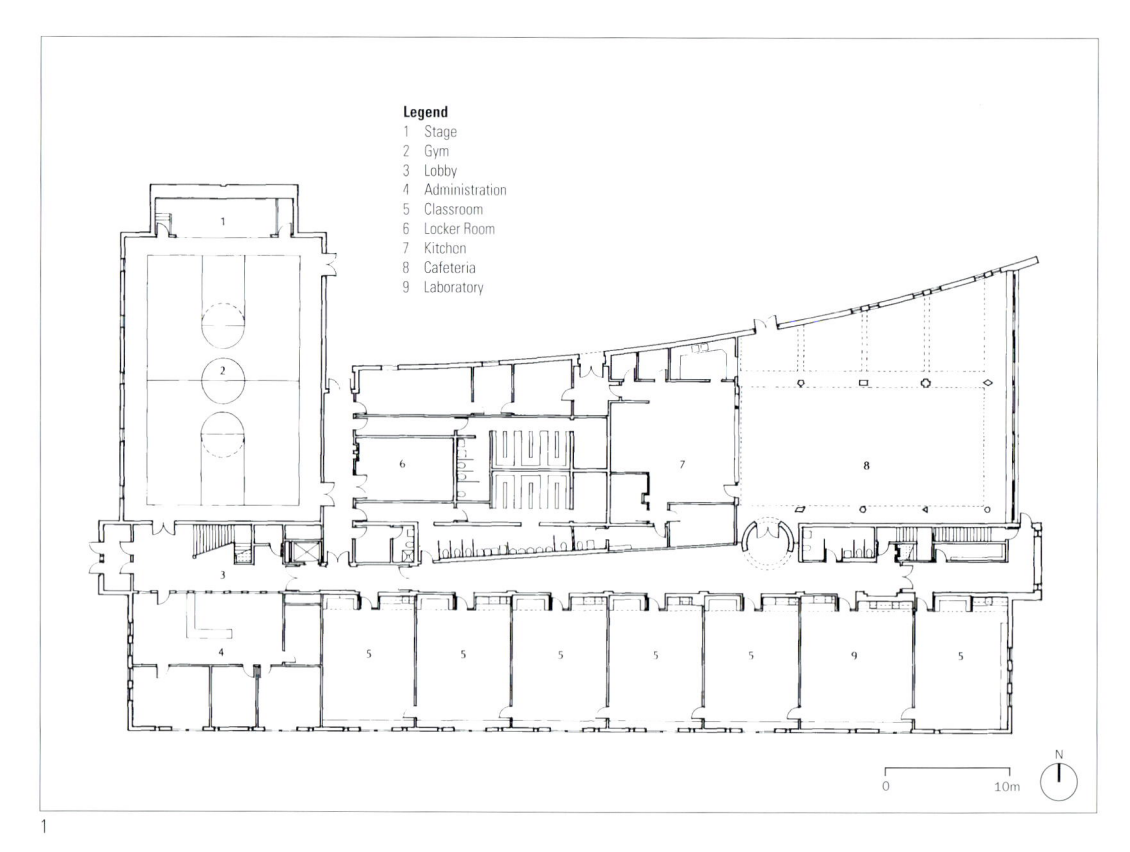

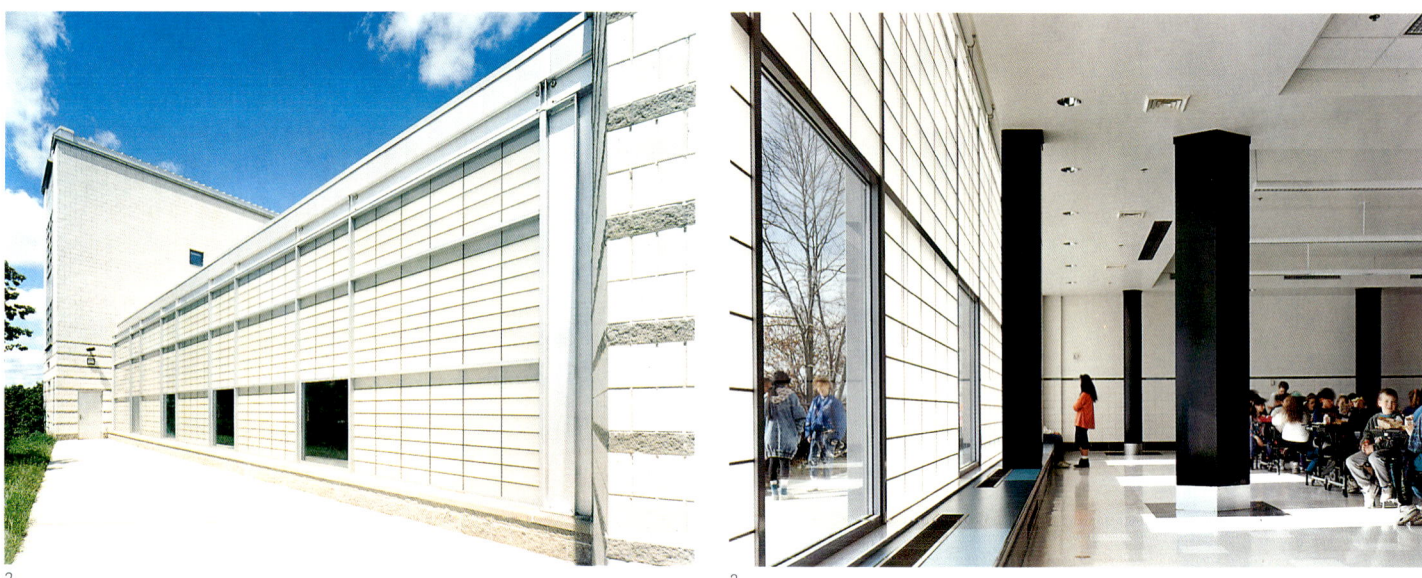

Legend
1 Stage
2 Gym
3 Lobby
4 Administration
5 Classroom
6 Locker Room
7 Kitchen
8 Cafeteria
9 Laboratory

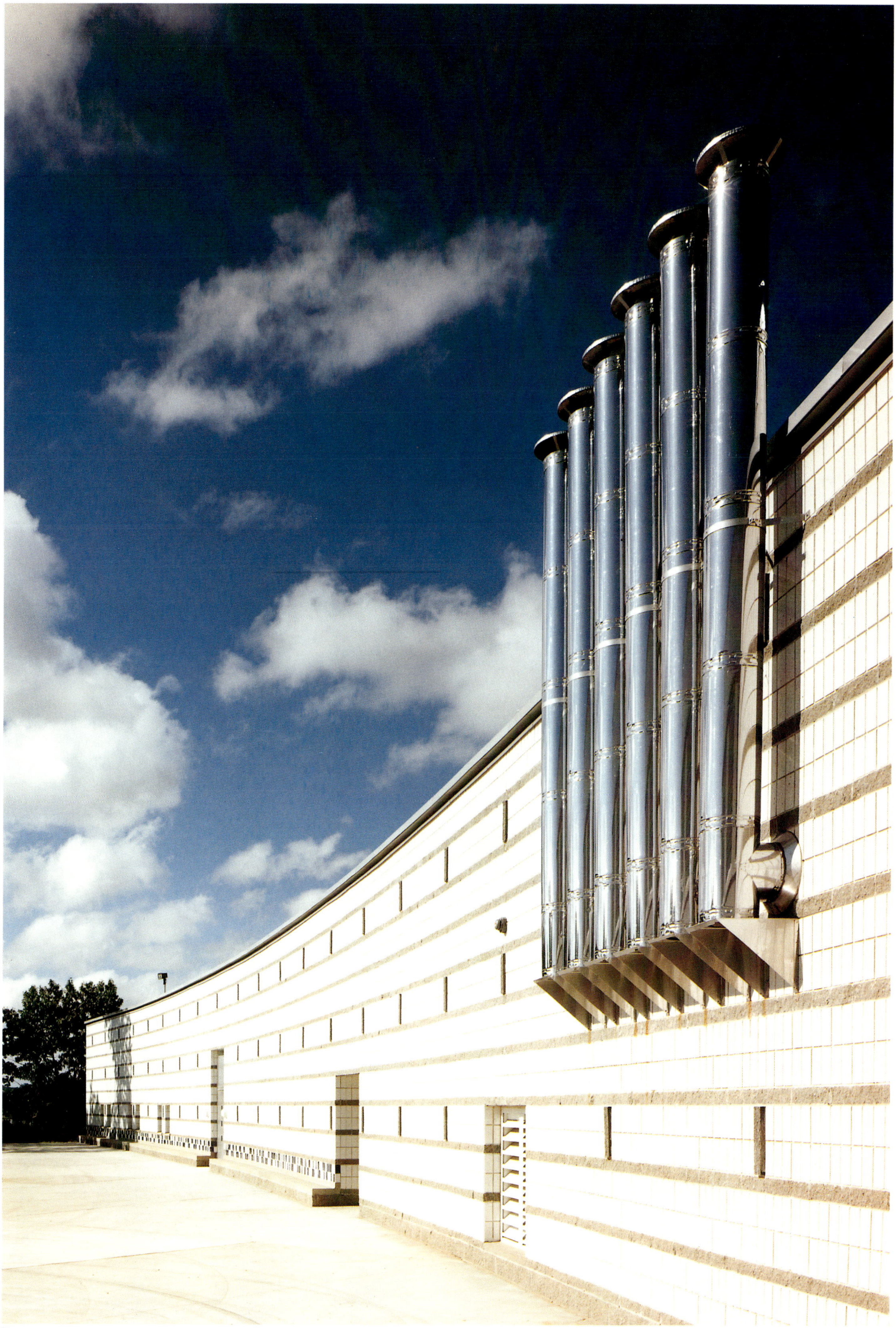

5

Strandschool
Tyresoe, Sweden
Birgitta Holm Arkitektkontor AB

1 Building from west
2 Entrance from southwest
3 Upper main corridor to north east
4 Communication in learning area
5 Ground floor plan
6 Part of general learning area

Photo credit: courtesy Birgitta Holm Arkitektkontor AB

Primary and Secondary Education **35**

Easton Intermediate School
Easton, Massachusetts, USA
Earl R. Flansburgh + Associates, Inc

1   First floor plan
2   Lighted cupolas mark the school entries
3   Cafeteria can be used for special events
4   Spacious interior lobbies connect the school's functions
5   Stage in gym encourages multi-use
6   Five sided classrooms facilitate different furniture arrangements

Photo credit: Steve Rosenthal

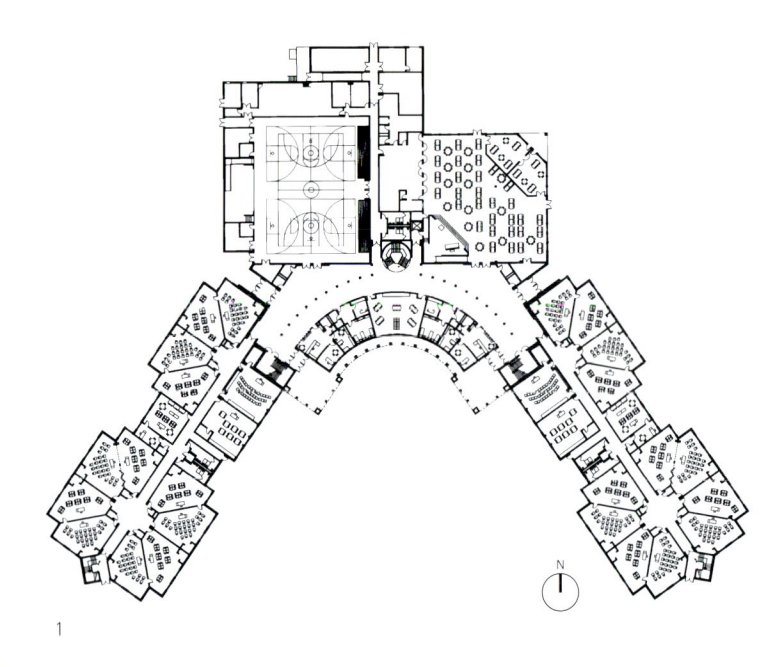

Primary and Secondary Education

1

2

3

4

Essling Secondary School
Vienna, Austria
Günter Domenig

1 Classroom section 'the Point'
2 Stairs down from the main hall to gyms
3 Side view of dining hall/event hall
4 Schoolyard with arena

Photo credit: Paul Ott

Iwadeyama Junior High School
Japan
Riken Yamamoto & Field Shop
1 Exterior view of gymnasium and Wing of Wind
2&3 View from the student lounge
4 Situated between classroom and laboratory is media gallery
Opposite:
Media Gallery
Photo credit: Mitsumasa Fujitsuka

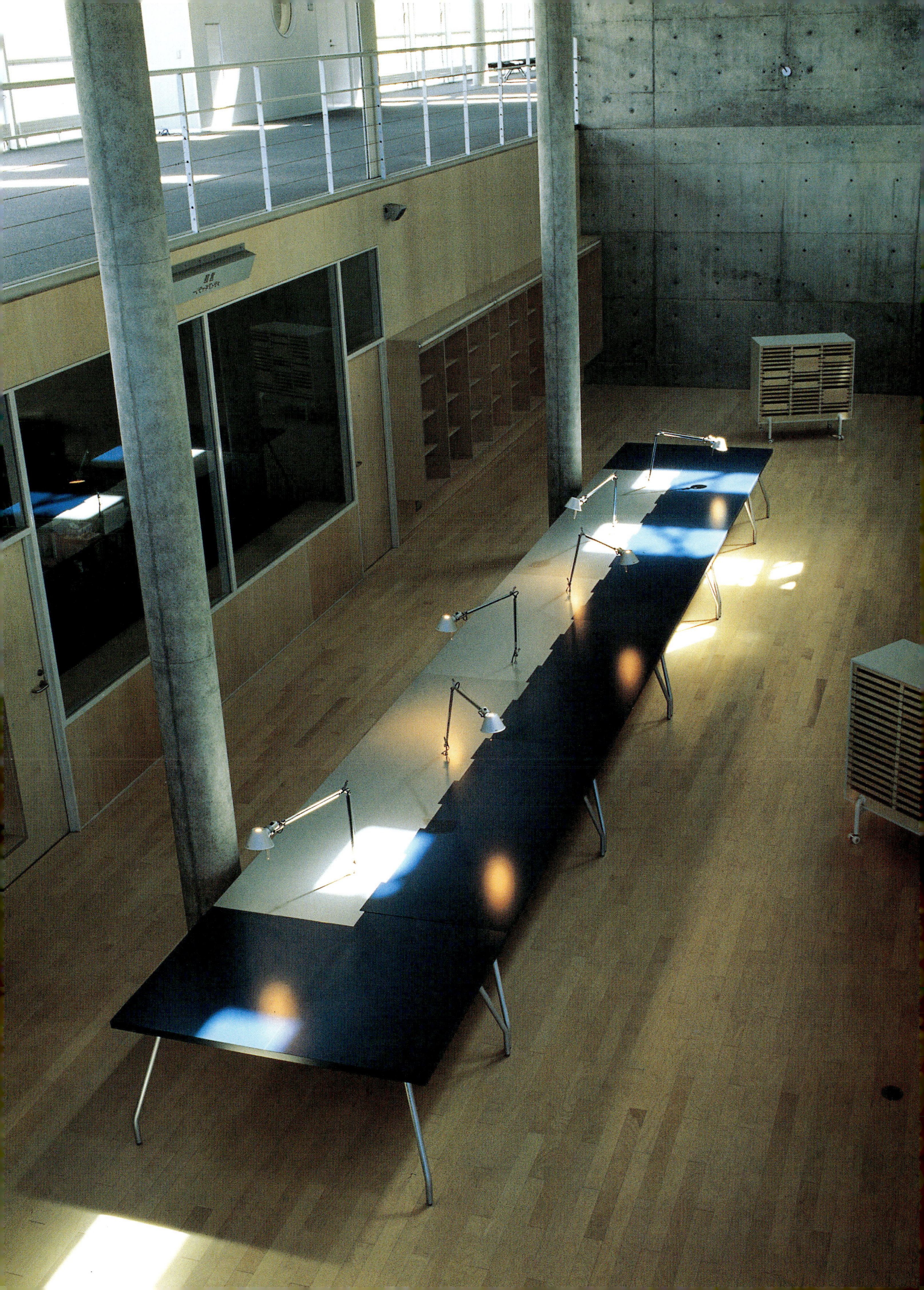

Pingry School
Bernards Township, New Jersey, USA
Hardy Holzman Pfeiffer Associates

1 Rear facade
2 Entrance facade
3 Clocktower at entrance facade
4 Common area at lowest level of lobby
5 View of lobby from library level
Photo credit: Norm McGrath

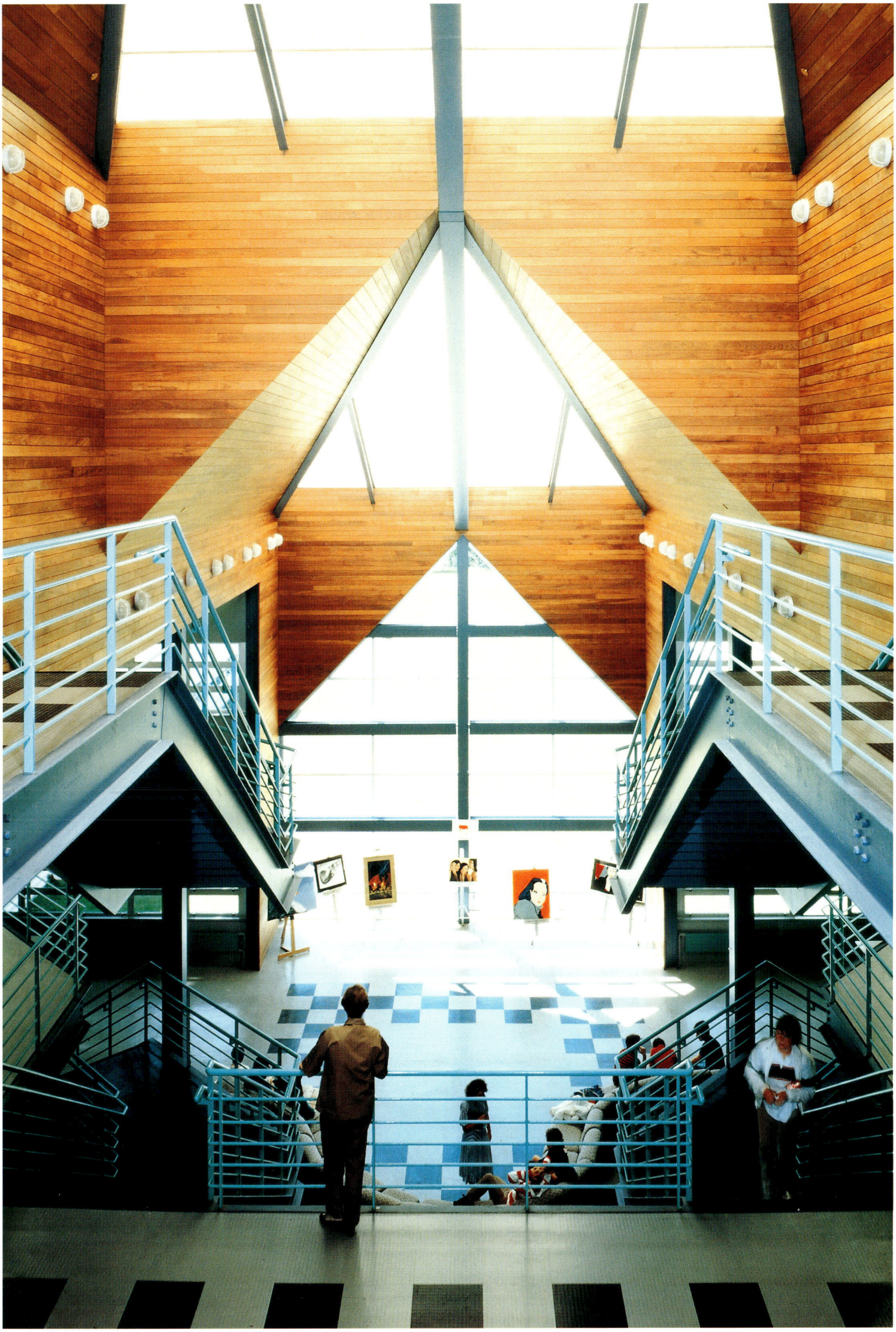

5

**Mount Pleasant Elementary School
Nashua, New Hampshire, USA**
TAMS Consultants, Inc.
1   West elevation, gym/art room
2   East elevation, front
3   Library interior
Photo credit: William T. Smith

**Boston College High School Library
Boston, Massachusetts, USA**
Tsoi/Kobus & Associates Architects
4   Reference area and circulation desk
5   Reading room
Photo credit: Steve Rosenthal

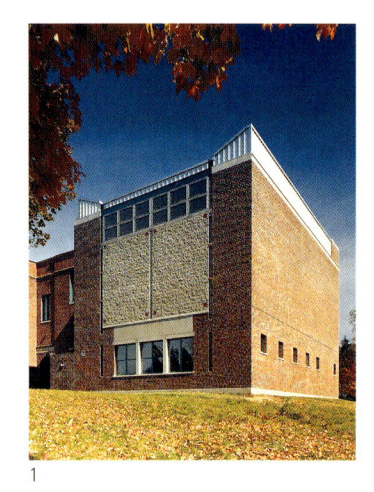

4

5

Primary and Secondary Education 45

Toowoomba Grammar School
Toowoomba, Queensland, Australia
Powell Dods & Thorpe

1. Paths lead to large covered play areas
2. Utilising 1890s architectural style
3. L.T. Heenan Science and Technology Laboratories
4. Leafy aspects for the cricket and rugby pavilion
5. Modern facilities and an interactive learning environment

Photo credit: courtesy Powell Dods & Thorpe

Primary and Secondary Education

**Student Recreation Center,
Miss Porter's School
Farmington, Connecticut, USA**
Tai Soo Kim Partners, Architects

1 Elevated running track enjoys skylight and clerestory windows
2 Multi-purpose student lounge opens onto viewing deck/running track
3 Small scale building faces interior campus
4 Large field house is capped by skylight and copper roofing
5 Daylight filled gymnasium has multi-purpose flooring

Photo credit: Robert Benson Photography

Primary and Secondary Education

Salisbury Upper School
Salisbury, Maryland, USA
Hardy Holzman Pfeiffer Associates

1   Site plan
2   View of northwest corner of building
3   Interior of salt dome with entrance to administration area at ground level
4   View of library on second level of salt dome
5   Interior view of connector between classrooms and library
6   View of main entrance

Photo credit: David Franzen

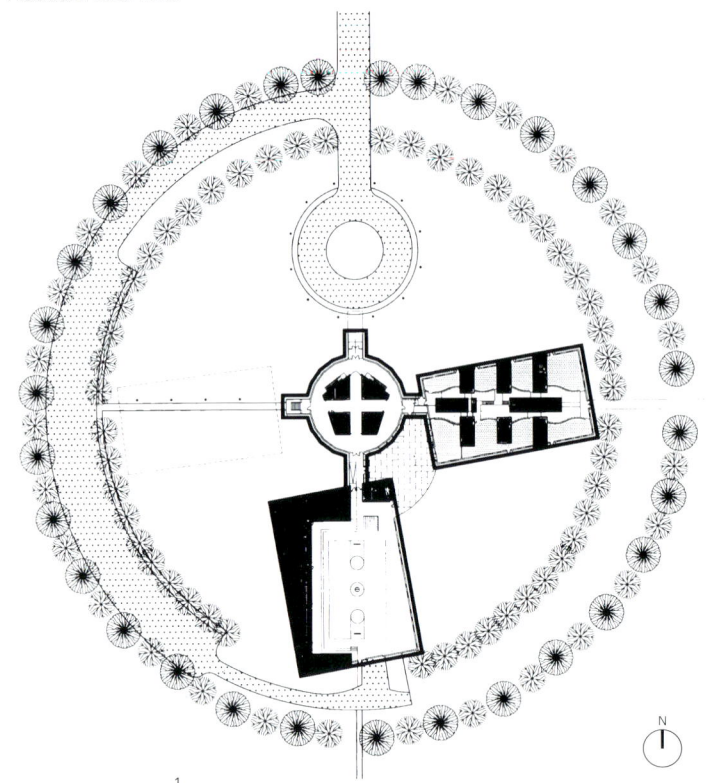

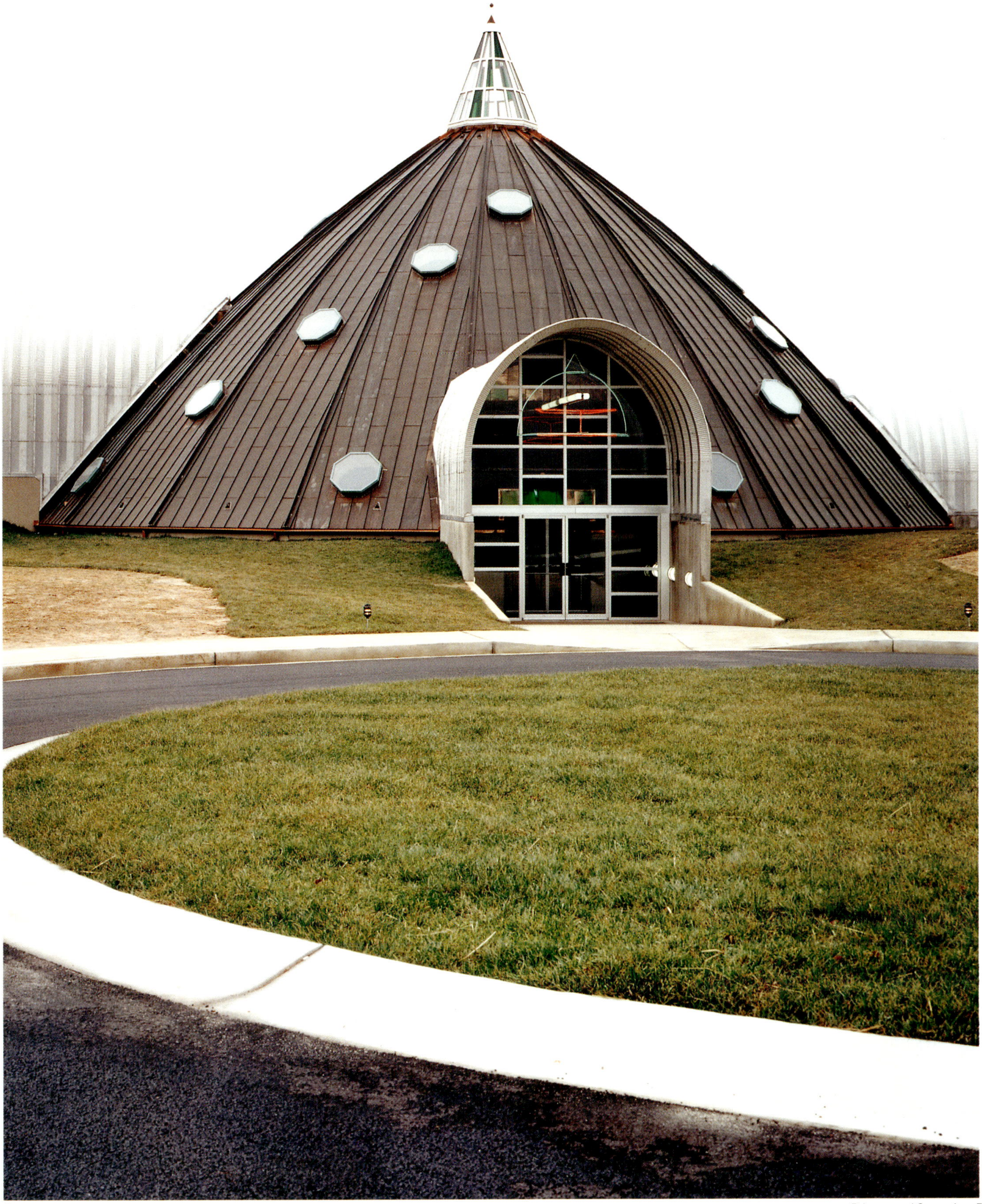

6

Paseo Academy of Visual & Performing Arts, Shared Facility and Middle School
Kansas City, Missouri, USA
WRS Architects, Inc.

1. Main floor plan
2. Lobby is accentuated by a dramatic bridge accessing theatre balcony
3. Shared facility prominently marks the corner entrance to the 'L' shaped complex
4. Student exhibition gallery provides a forum for public display of student art work
5. Recital hall proscenium

Photo credit: Paul Brokering

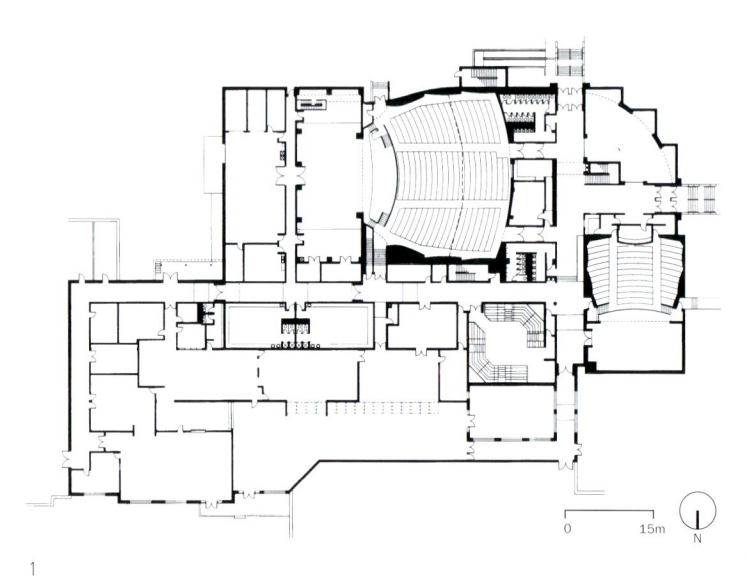

4

5

Craft Design Technology Studios
Bryanston School
Blandford, Dorset, UK
CZWG Architects

1 Ground floor plan
2 Northwest and southwest elevation from west
3 View across courtyard
4 Norman Shaw Building that dictated the ensuing design
5 Northeast elevation
6 Front elevation showing main entrance across courtyard

Photo credit: Jo Reid and John Peck

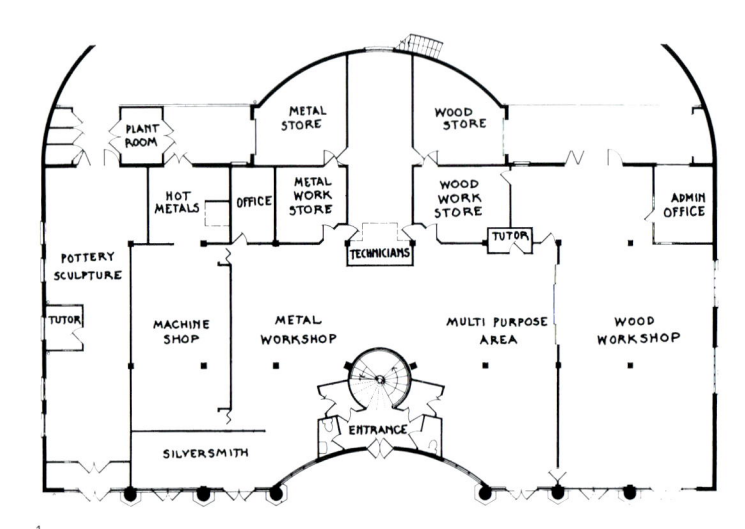

5

6

*"Build today, then strong and sure,
With a rim and ample base;
And ascending and secure
Shall tomorrow find its place"*
– Henry Wadsworth Longfellow

Adult Education Spaces

Lycée Albert Camus in Fréjus
Fréjus, France
Foster and Partners
1–3 Exterior
4 Interior
Photo credit: courtesy Foster and Partners

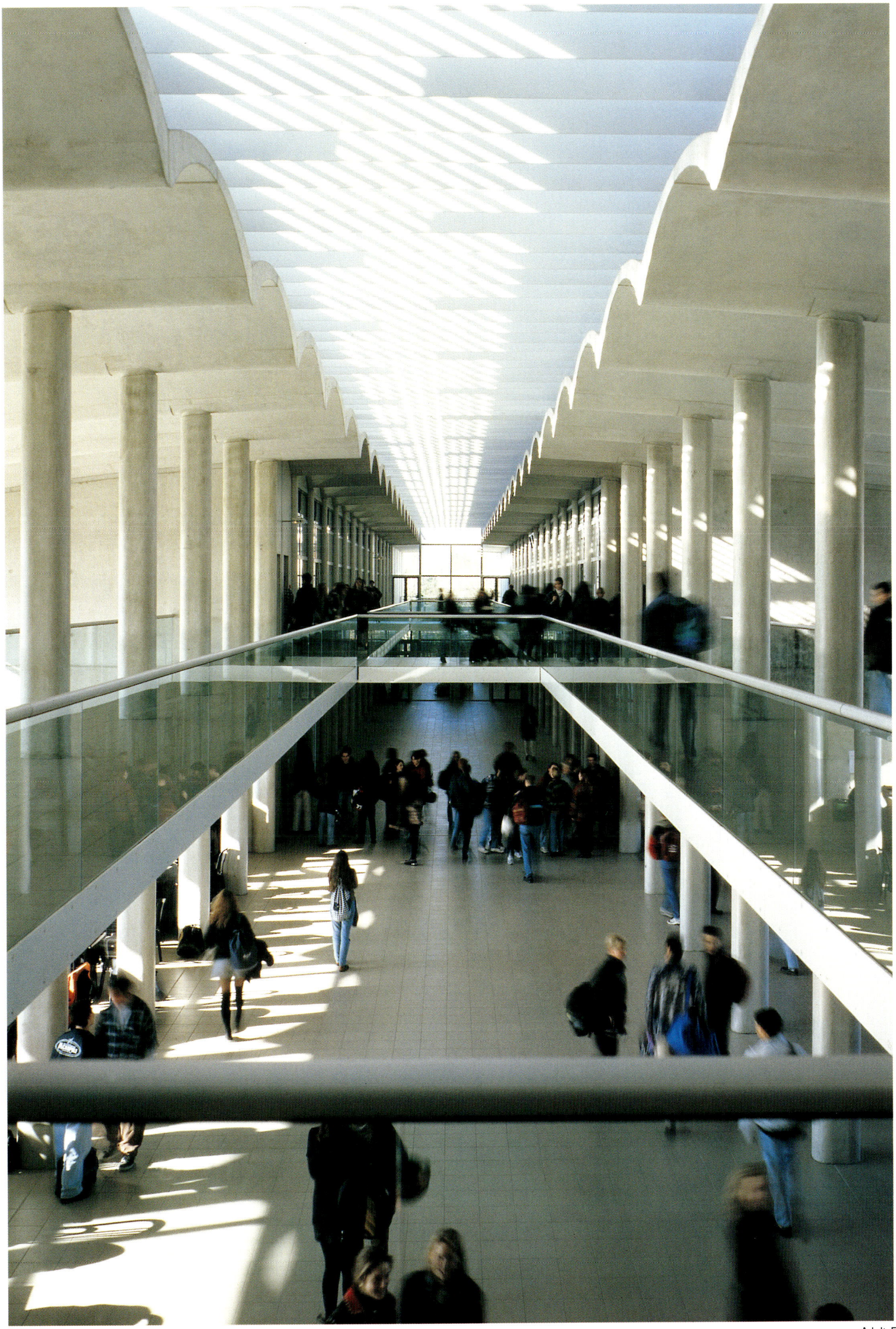

4

**University of Northern Colorado,
Gunter Hall Renovation**
Greeley, Colorado, USA
Fentress Bradburn Architects
1   Rear elevation
2   Detail of entry
3   Classroom
4   Atrium
Following Page:
    Classroom with old windows
Photo credit: Nick Merrick/Hedrich Blessing,
Gordon Schenck

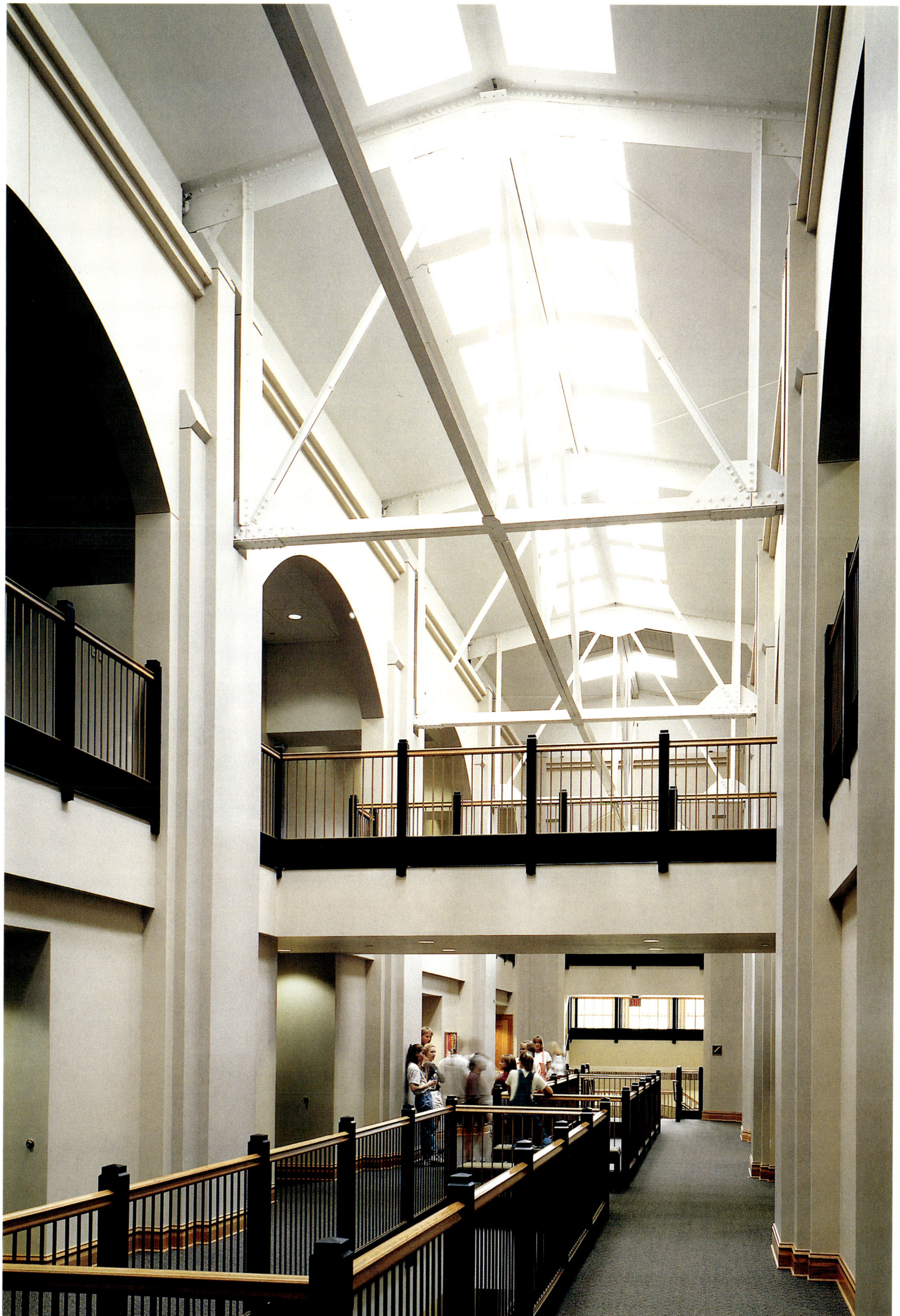

4

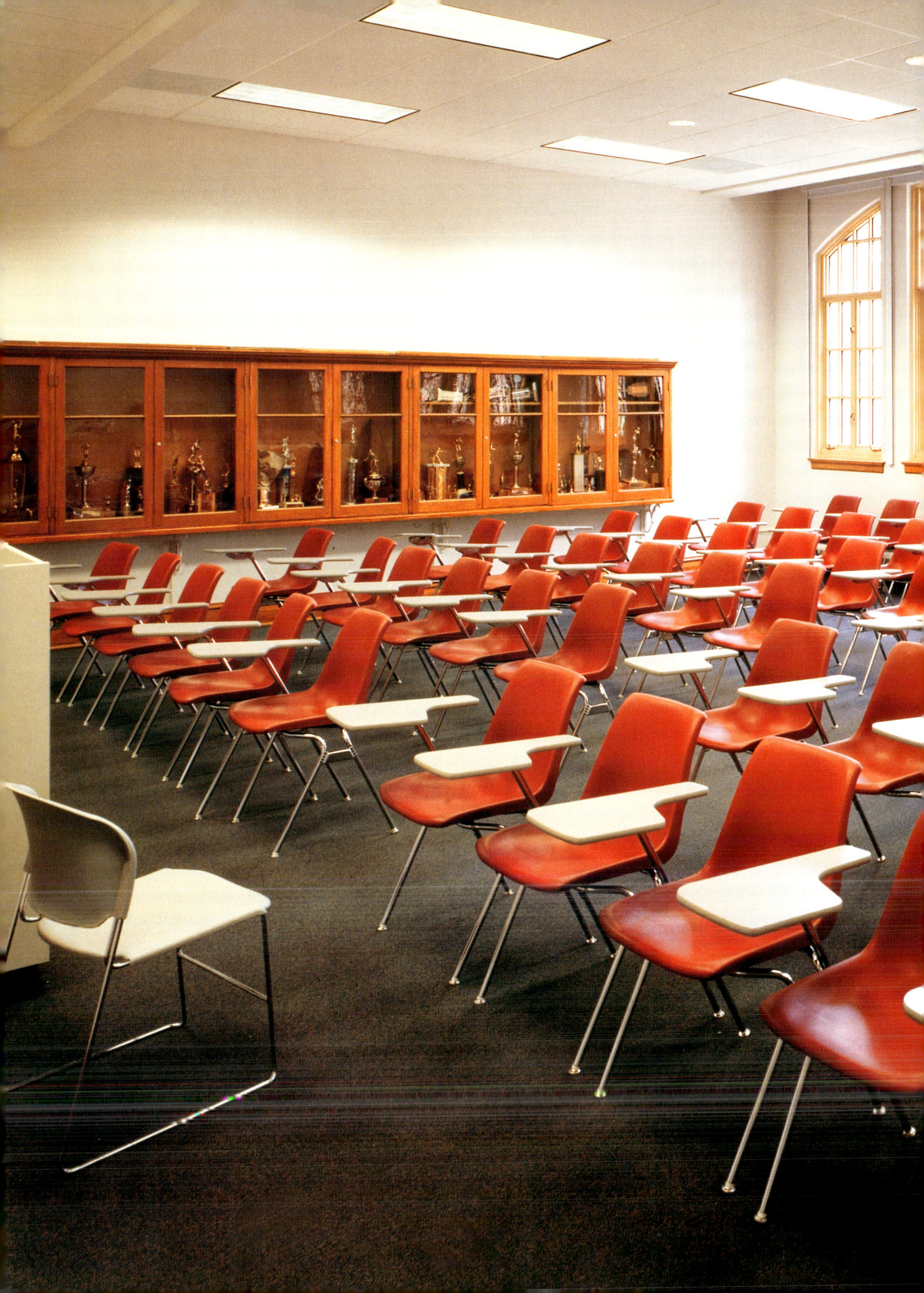

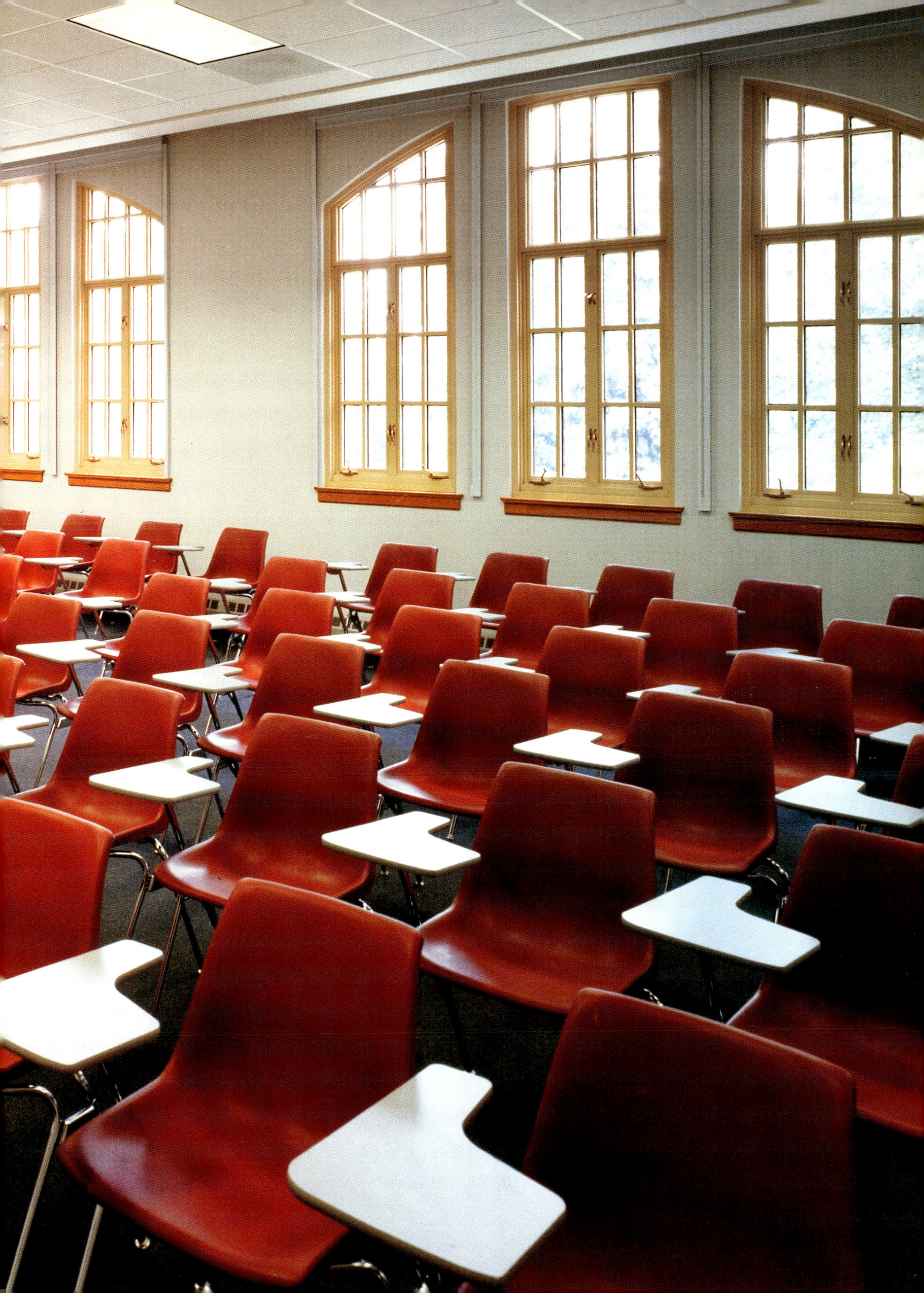

College of Wooster Ebert Art Center
Wooster, Ohio, USA
R.M.Kliment & Frances Halsband Architects

1. First floor plan
2. View of façade of existing building and new wing from south
3. View from north
4. Drawing studio in former gymnasium space
5. Lecture hall second floor

Following Page:
  West gallery looking west (sculpture by Walter Zurko)
Photo credit: Cervin Robinson

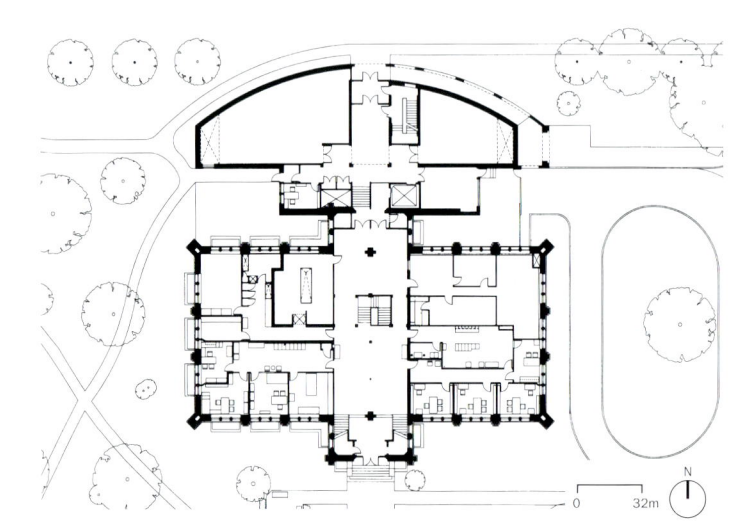

4

5

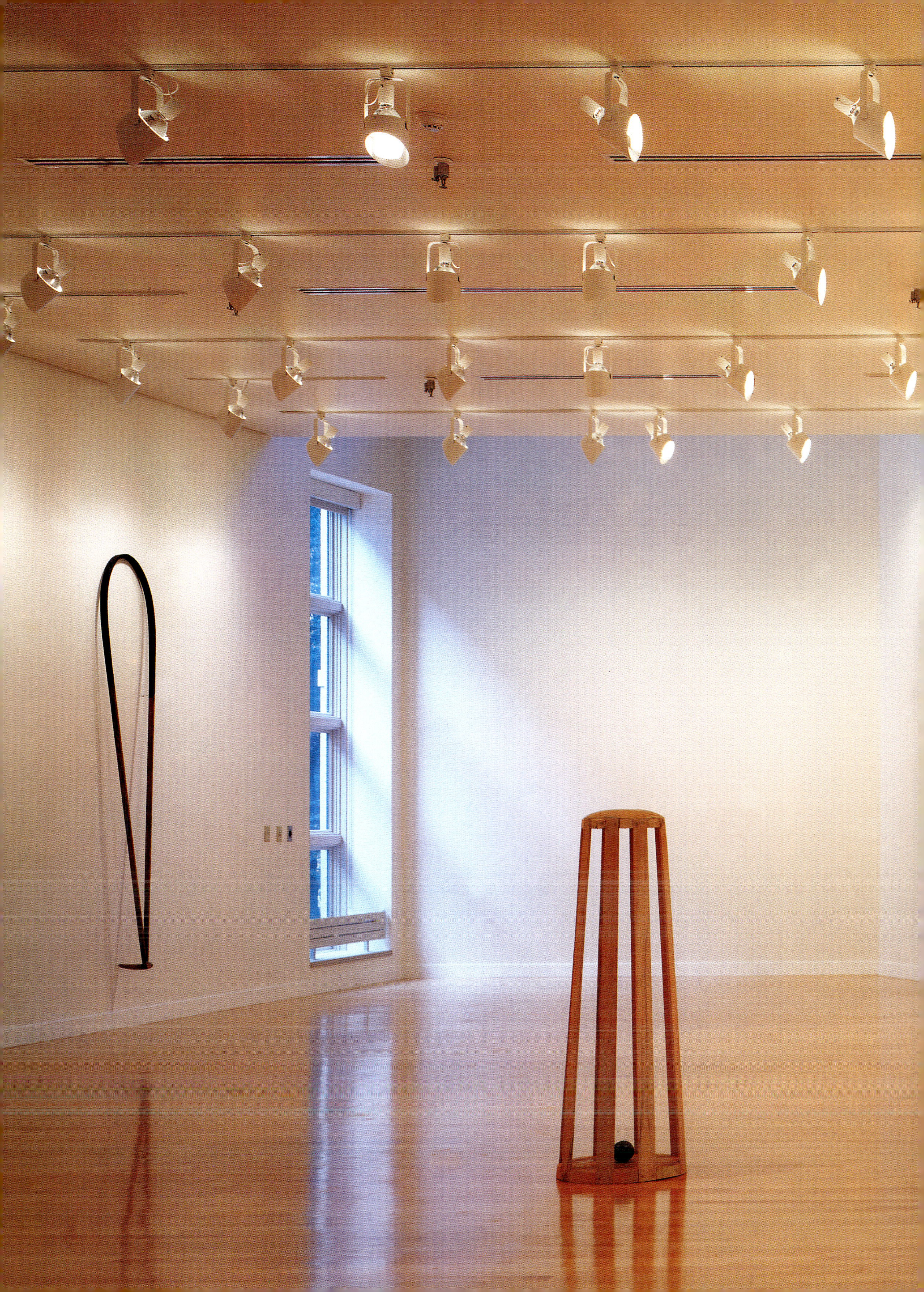

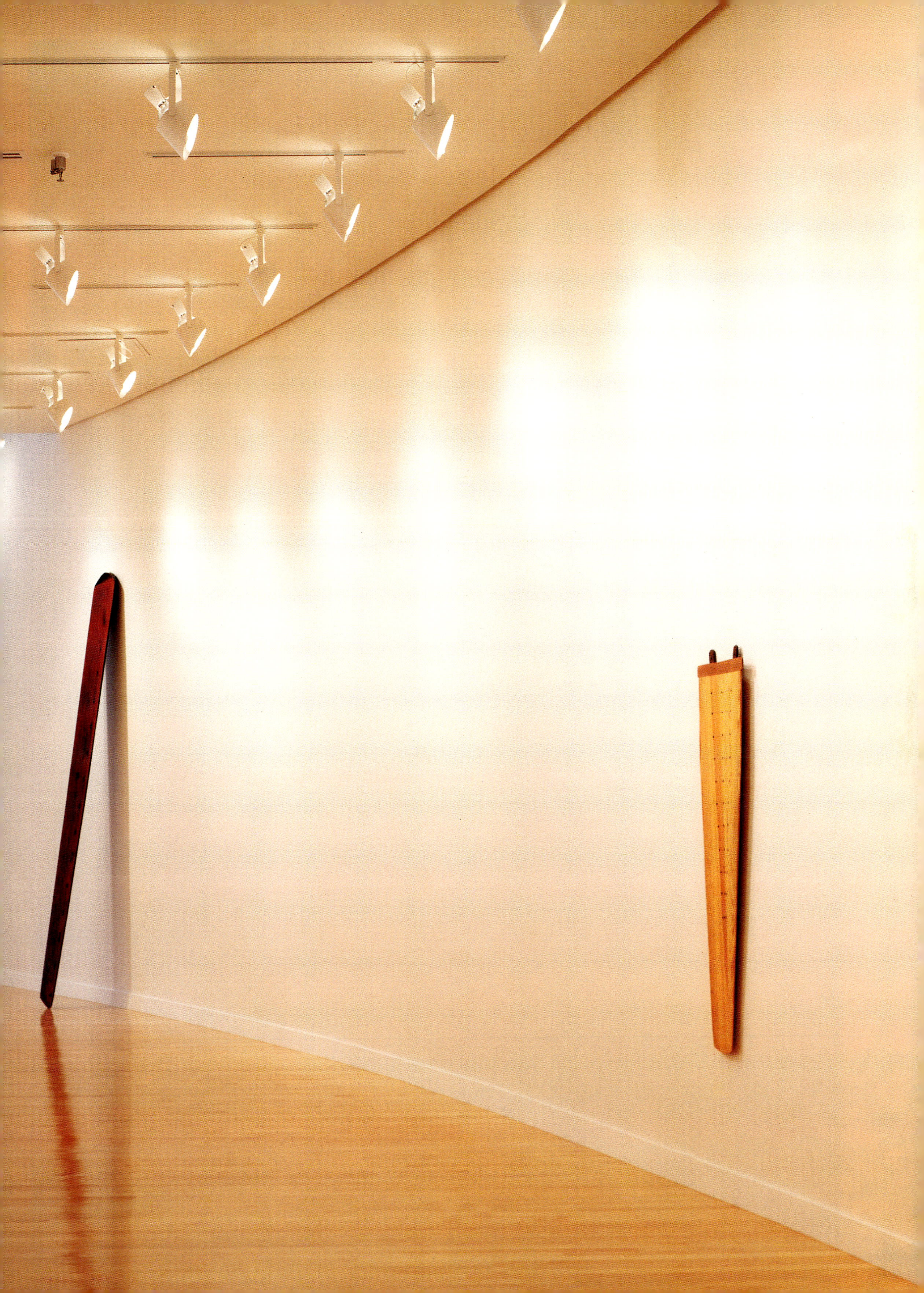

Center for the Arts, Middlebury College
Middlebury, Vermont, USA
Hardy Holzman Pfeiffer Associates
1　View of courtyard on east side of building with entrances to gallery and building
2　Building as seen from the northwest
3　Dance rehearsal studio
4　Second-level lobby looking towards rear entrance
5　Interior of 400-seat concert hall
Photo credit: Erik Borg (1); A. Blake Gardner (2); Norm McGrath (3–5)

Adult Education 69

National Museum of Wildlife Art
Jackson, Wyoming, USA
Fentress Bradburn Architects

1   Auditorium
2   Exterior/dining viewing terrace
3   Two storey lobby space
4   Entry lobby accessing bookstore, library, auditorium and galleries

Following Page:
   Museum viewed from below

Photo credit: Nick Merrick/Hedrich Blessing, Timothy Hursley

3

4

Adult Education 71

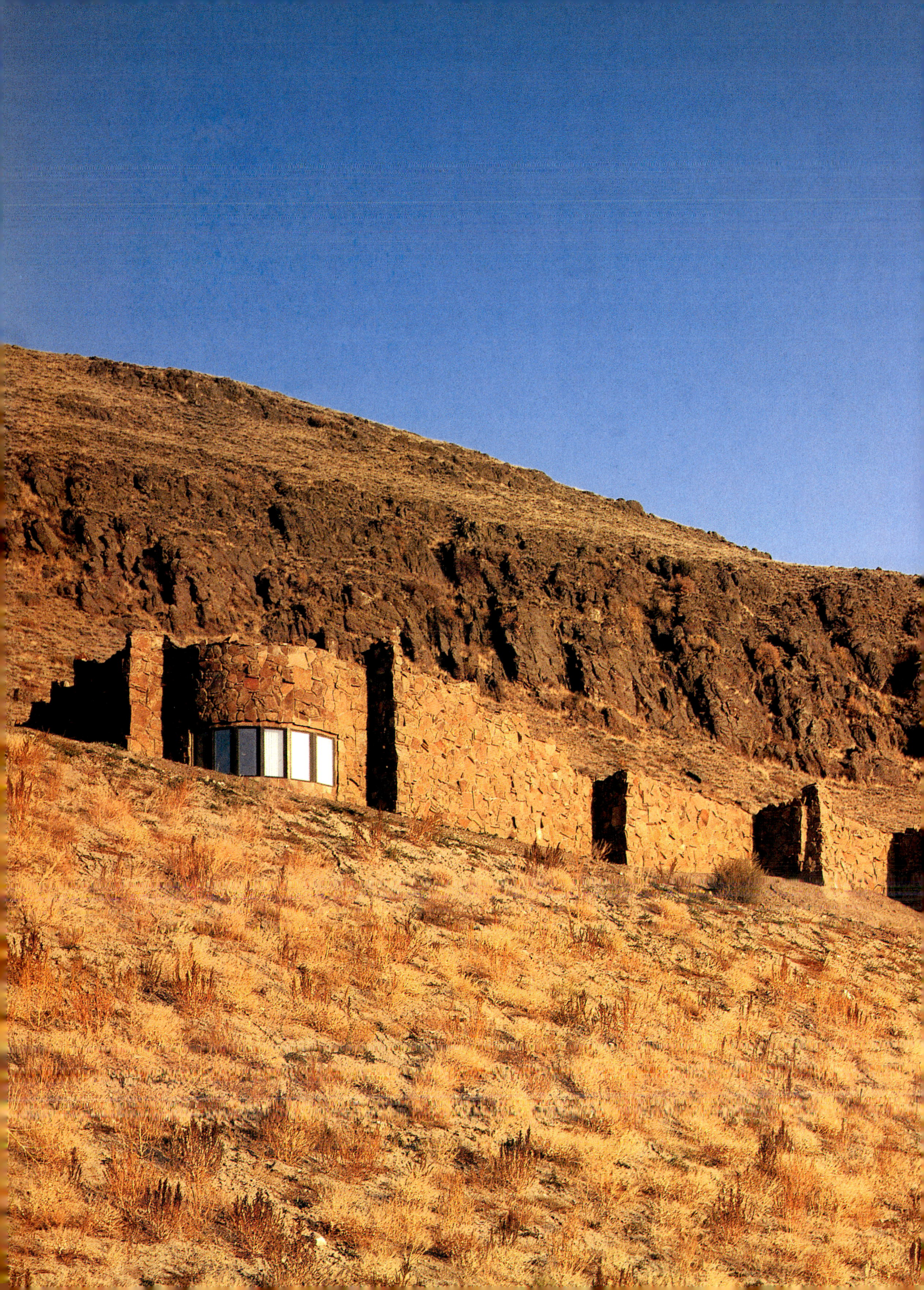

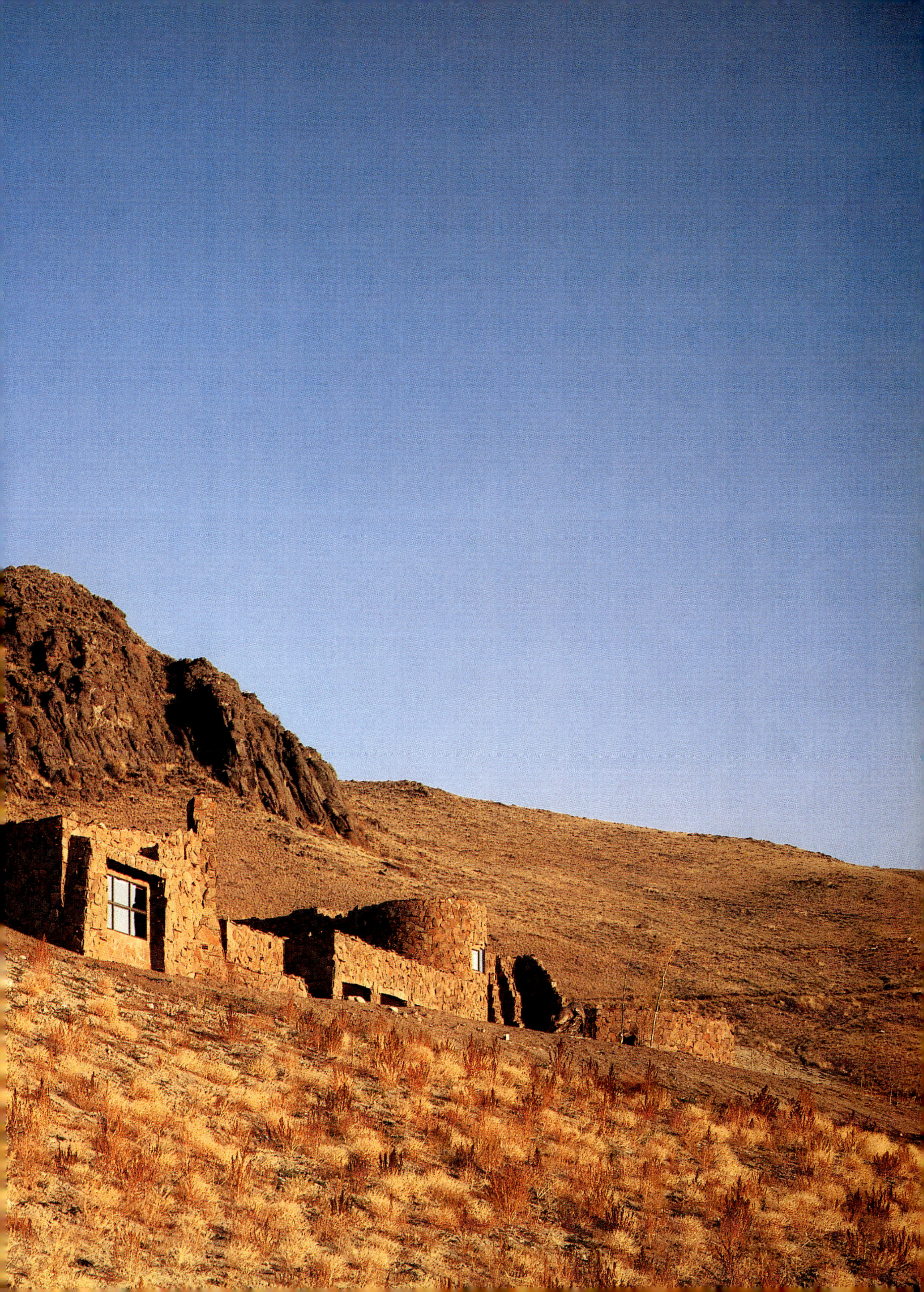

1

2

3

4

**Lied Education Center for the Arts,
Creighton University
Omaha, Nebraska, USA**
Hardy Holzman Pfeiffer Associates
1 Main entrance
2 Scene shop
3 Main entrance at night
4 Sculpture studio
5 Main gallery
Photo credit: Tom Kessler

Center for the Arts,
SUNY at Buffalo
Amherst, New York, USA
Gwathmey Siegel & Associates Architects
1 View of north facade overlooking Lake LaSalle
2 Atrium by day
3 Atrium from balcony lobby
4 View of public entrance and south facade from Coventry Circle
5 Orchestra and balcony lobbies by day
6 Atrium by night
Photo credit: Jeff Goldberg/Esto

5

6

**Center for the Arts,
SUNY at Buffalo**
Amherst, New York, USA
Gwathmey Siegel & Associates Architects

7&8 Dance studio with control room
and balcony overlooking dance floor
9 400-seat drama theatre
10 View from stage of main theatre

Photo credit: Jeff Goldberg/Esto

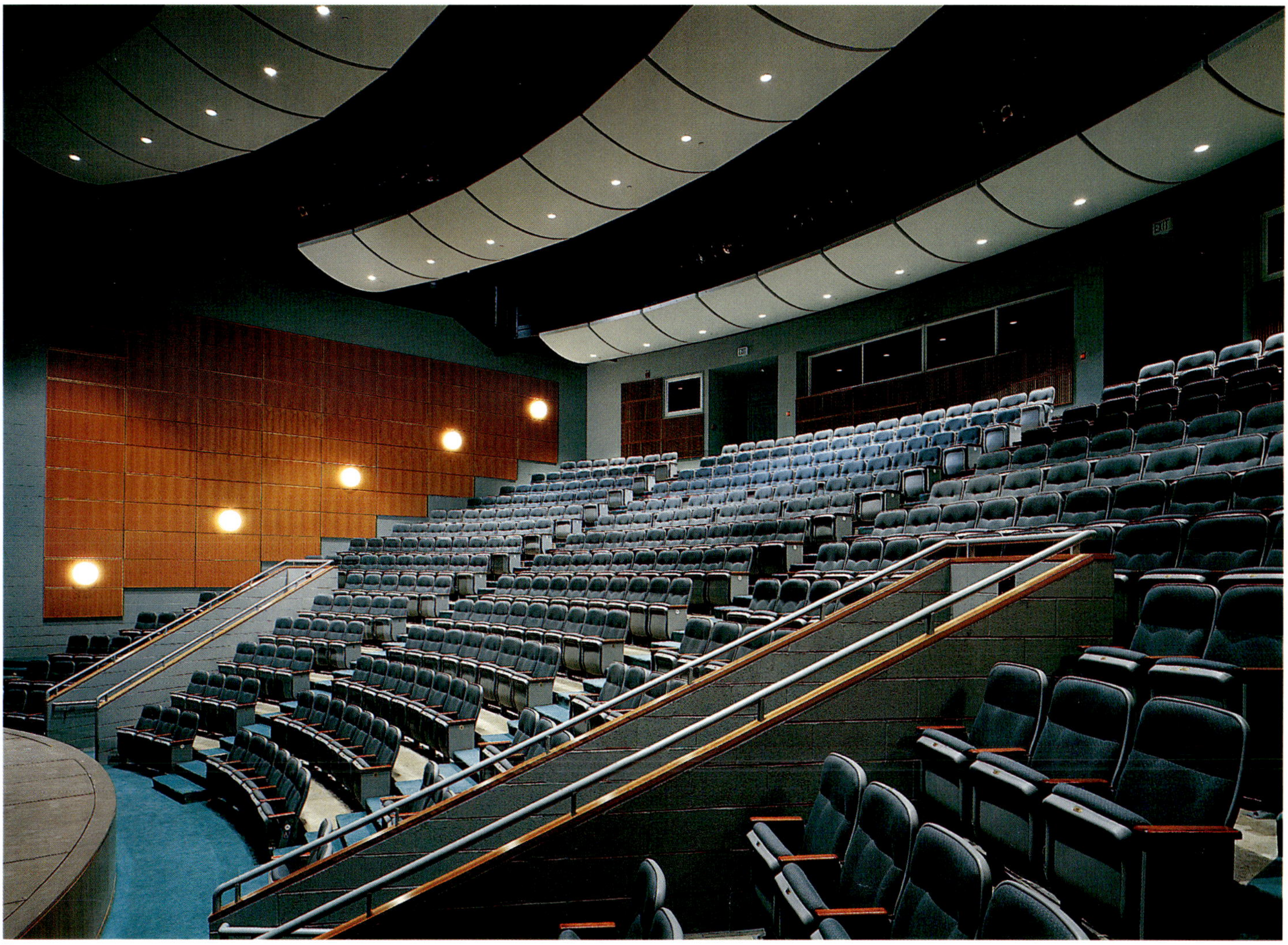

9

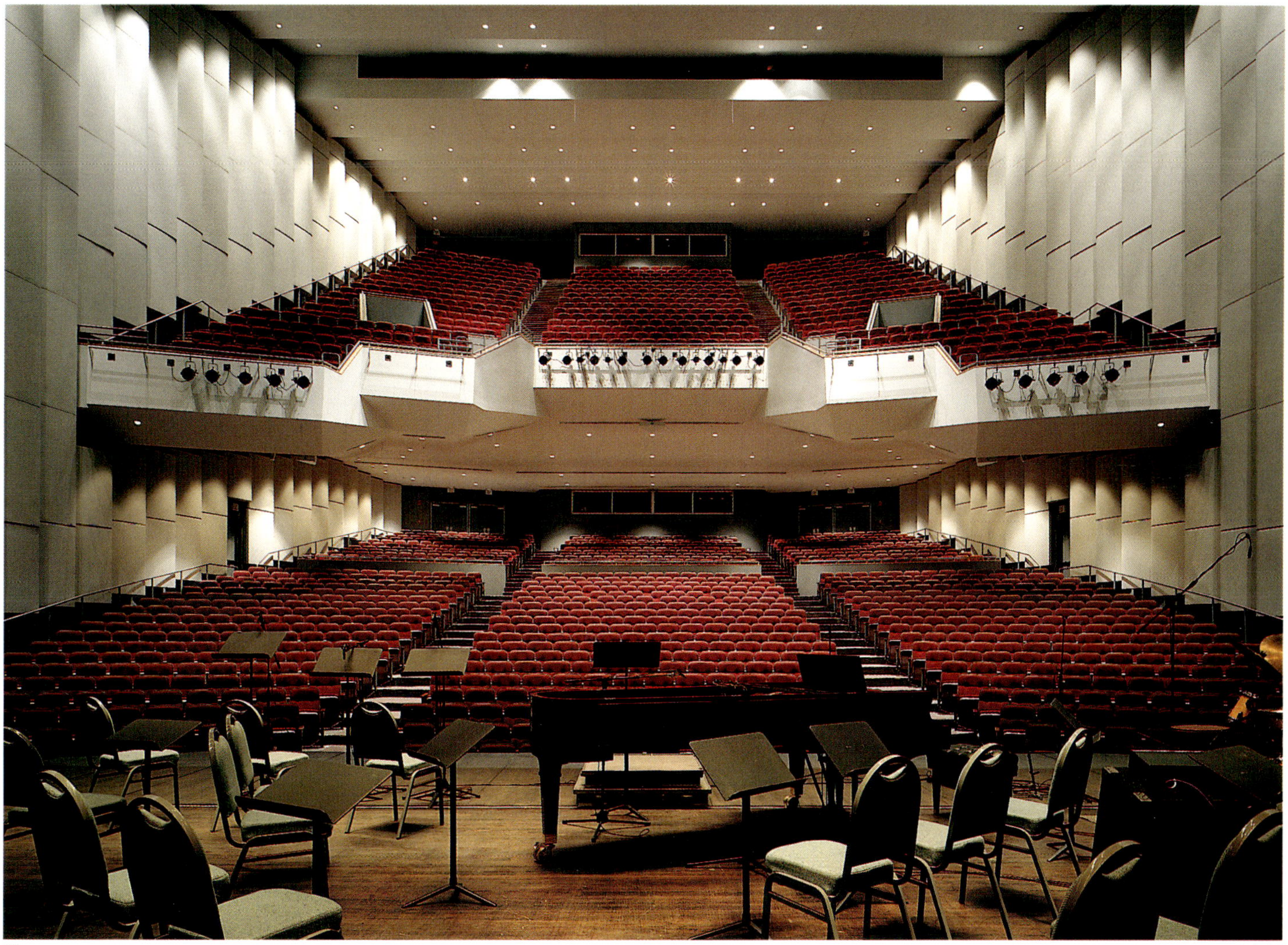

10

1

2

**Fine Arts Building, University of Nebraska
Omaha, Nebraska, USA**
Hardy Holzman Pfeiffer Associates
1 Main entrance
2 South facade
3 Main gallery
4 Painting studio
Photo credit: Tom Kessler

Adult Education 81

Music Facility
**University of California-Santa Cruz,
California, USA**
Antoine Predock Architect FAIA

1　First level floor plan
2　View from the Great Meadow
3　Upper plaza and connecting bridges over the courtyard and ravine
4　The ravine
5　Recital hall

Photo credit: courtesy Antoine Predock Architect FAIA

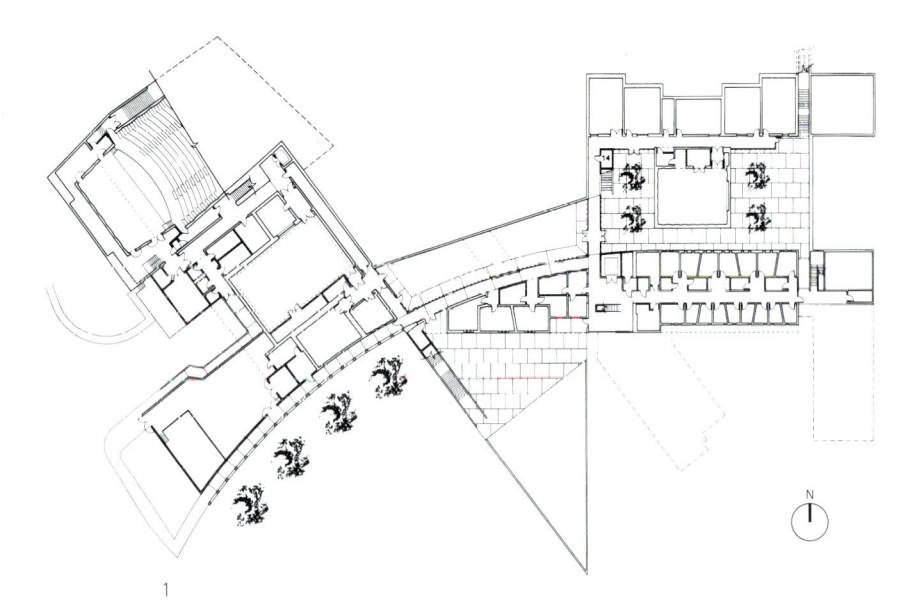

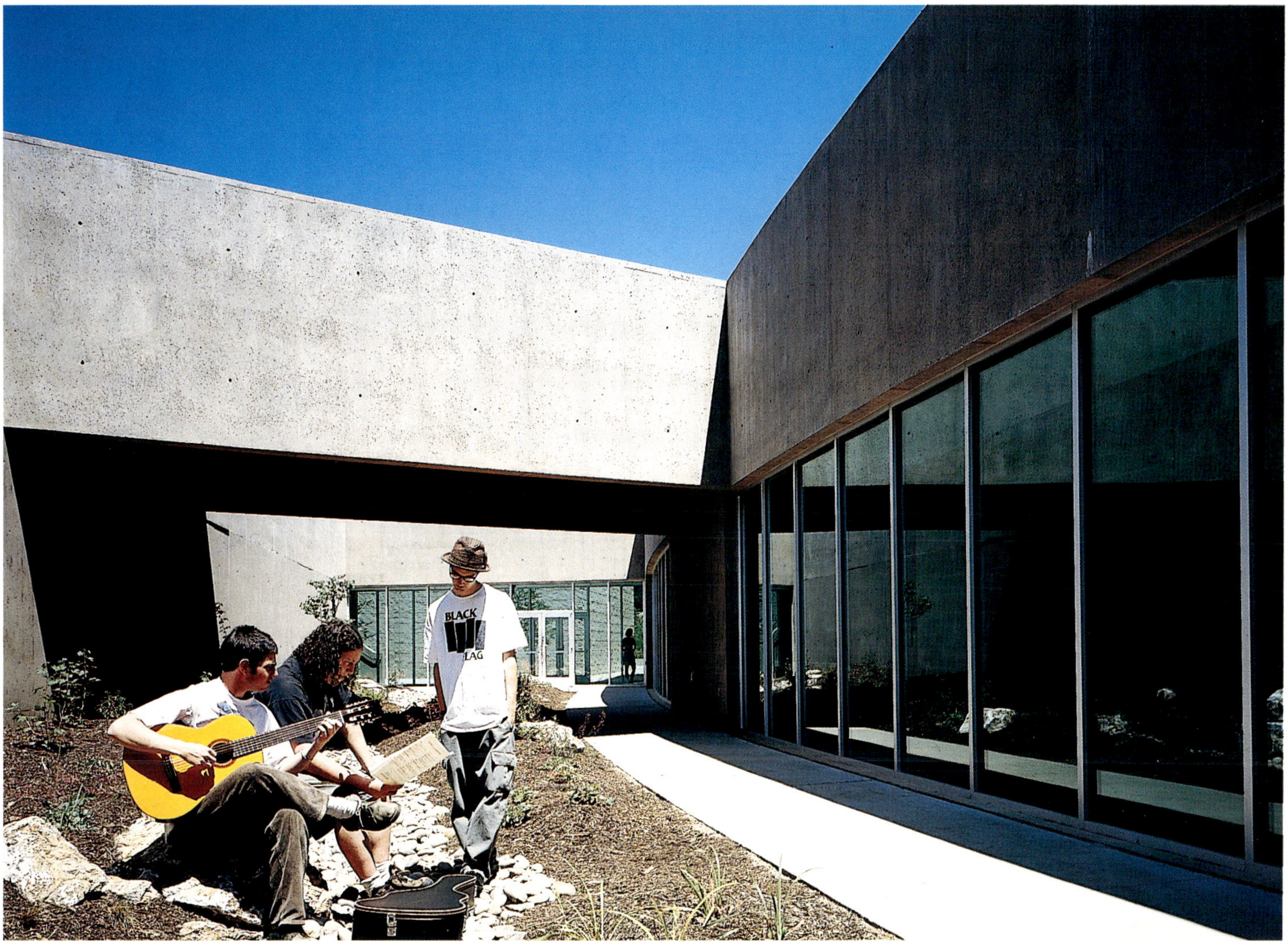

4

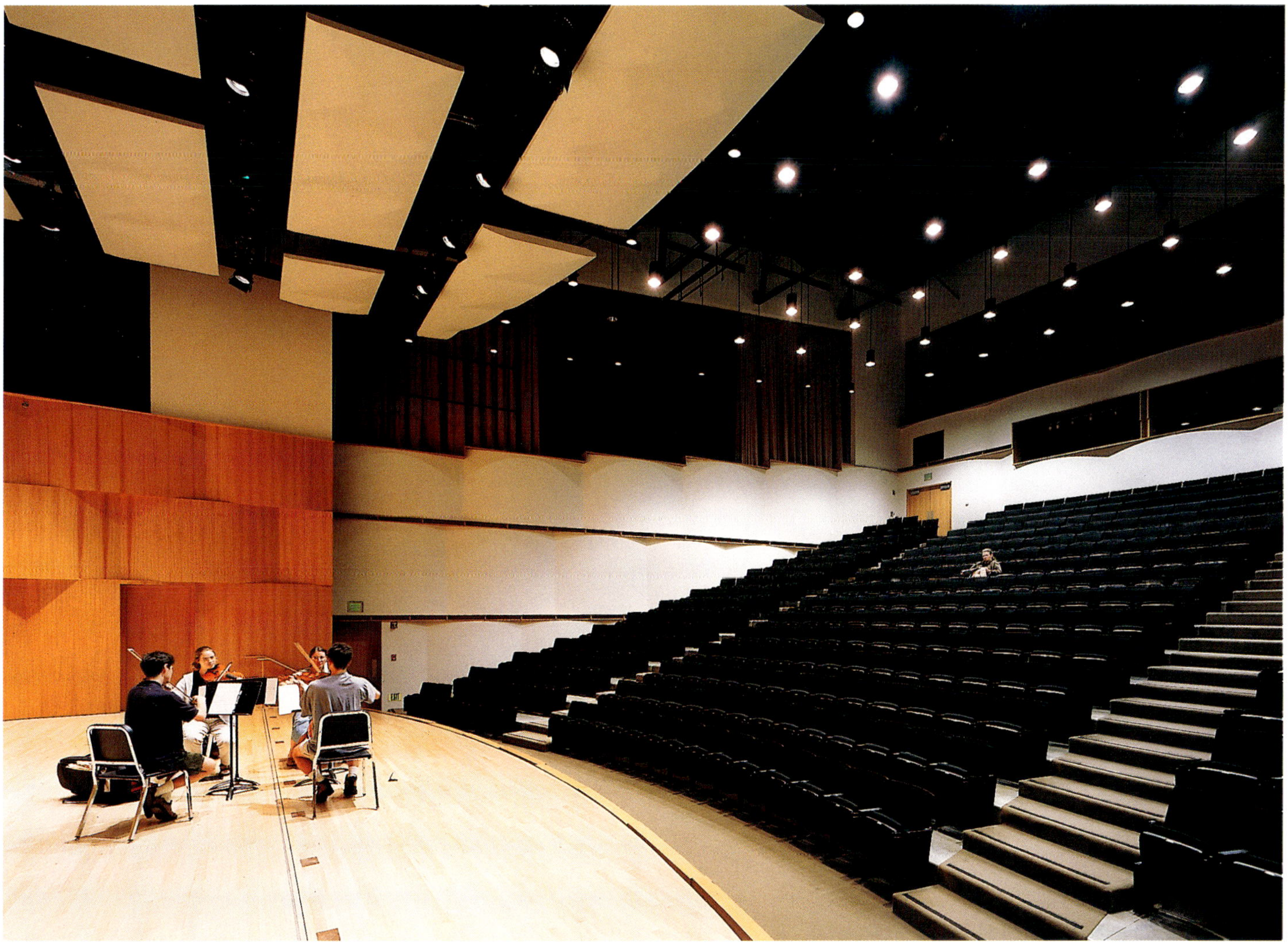
5

**Queensland Conservatorium of Music
Queensland, Australia**
Bligh Voller Nield Pty Ltd

1 Northern elevation to formal lawn
2 Main foyer space
3 Detail of main auditorium
4 Parklands entrance
5 Main auditorium space in concert mode
6 200 seat lecture/recital room

Photo credit: David Sandison

Adult Education 85

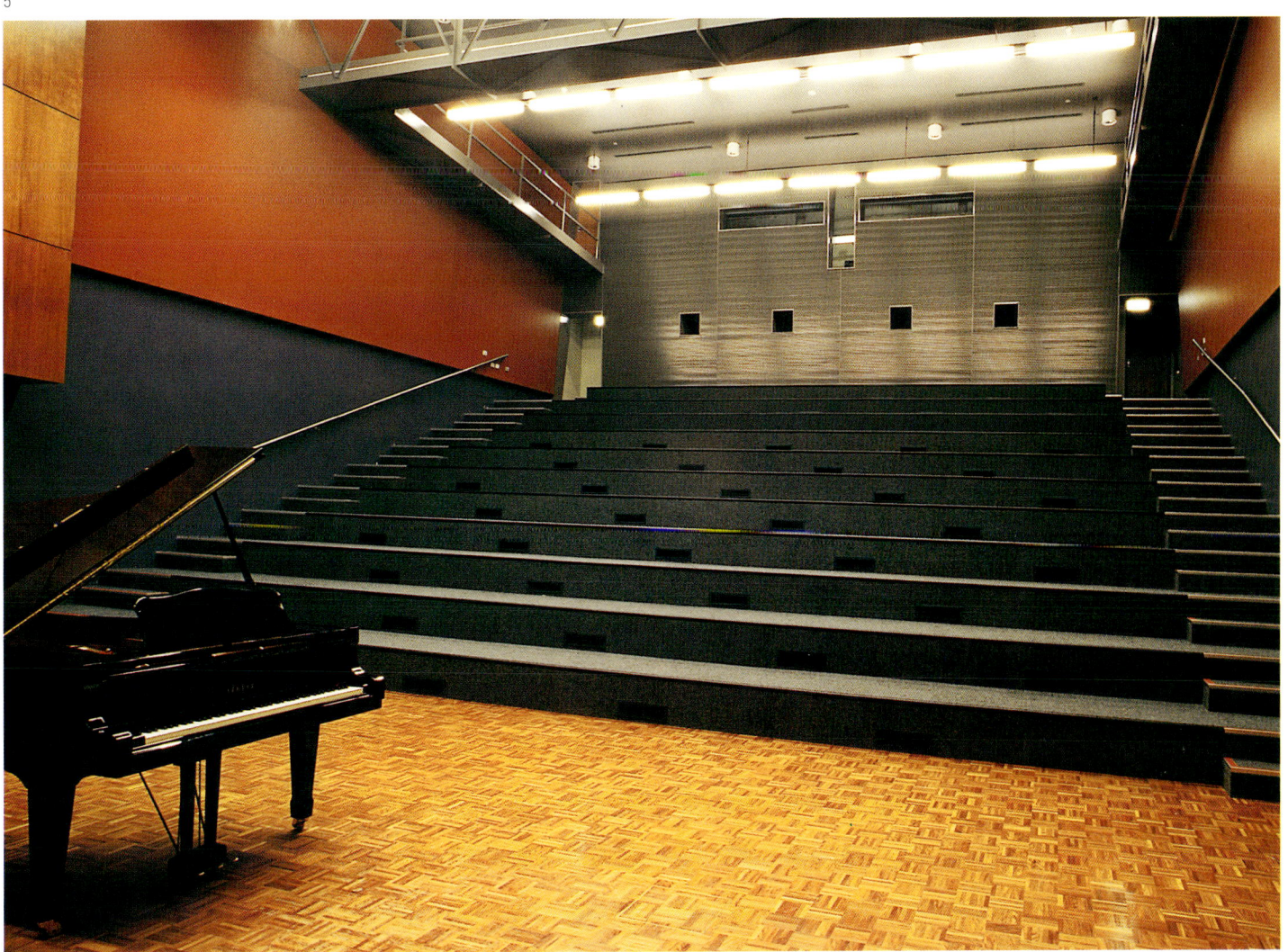

New Hall, University of Cambridge and Kaetsu Education and Cultural Centre
Cambridge, UK
Austin-Smith:Lord

1 Entrance to the Kaetsu Rotunda
2 Ramp approach to the Kaetsu Foyer
3 View from Huntington Road
4 The Kaetsu lecture and performance hall
5 The New Hall entrance to Rotunda

Photo credit: Alan Williams

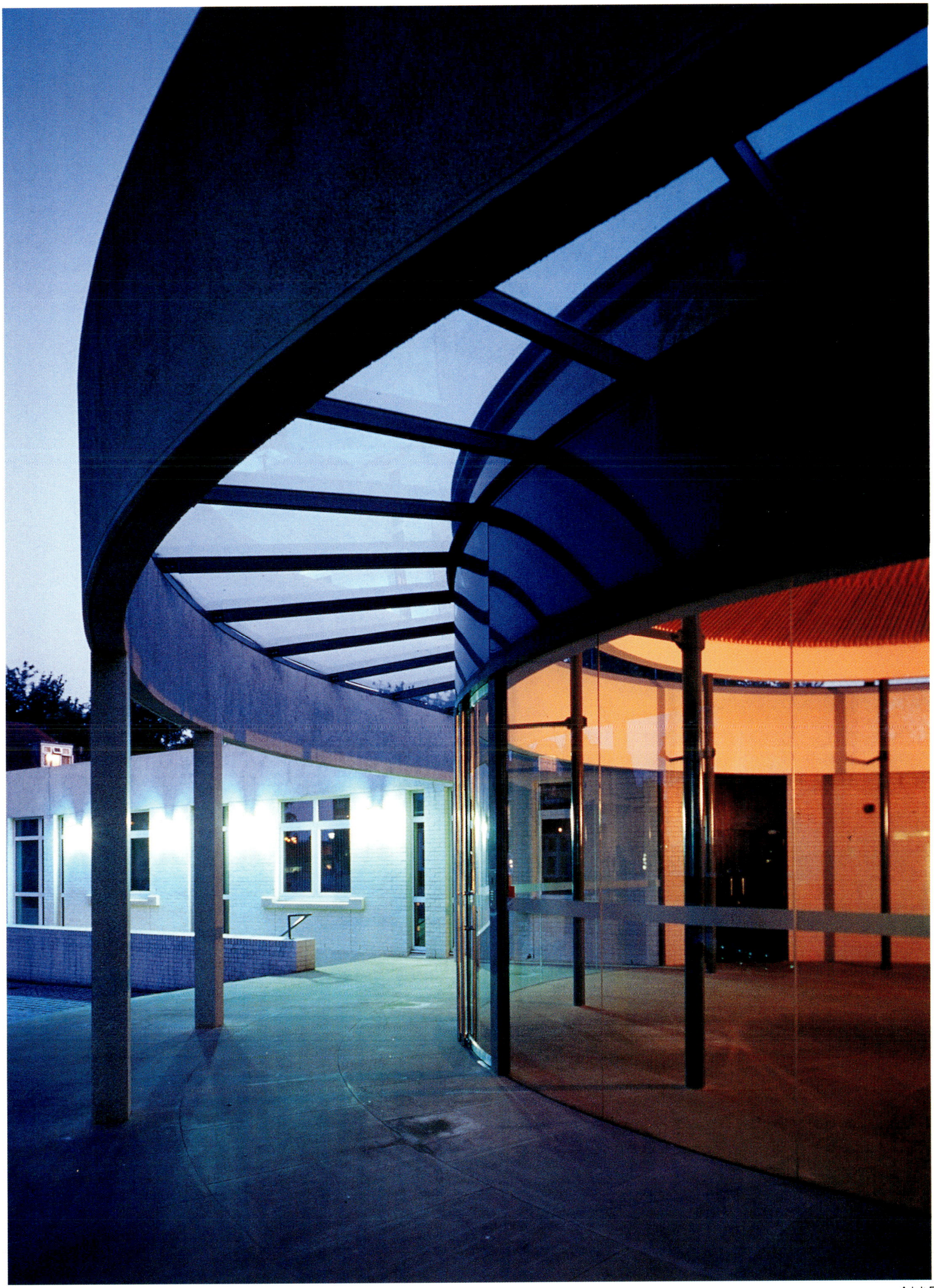

5

**Aboriginal and Islander Studies Centre,
James Cook University of North Queensland
Townsville, Queensland, Australia**
Macks & Robinson Pty Ltd
1 Plan
2 View from north (entrance)
3 Entrance lobby
4 Central courtyard
Photo credit: courtesy Macks & Robinson Pty Ltd

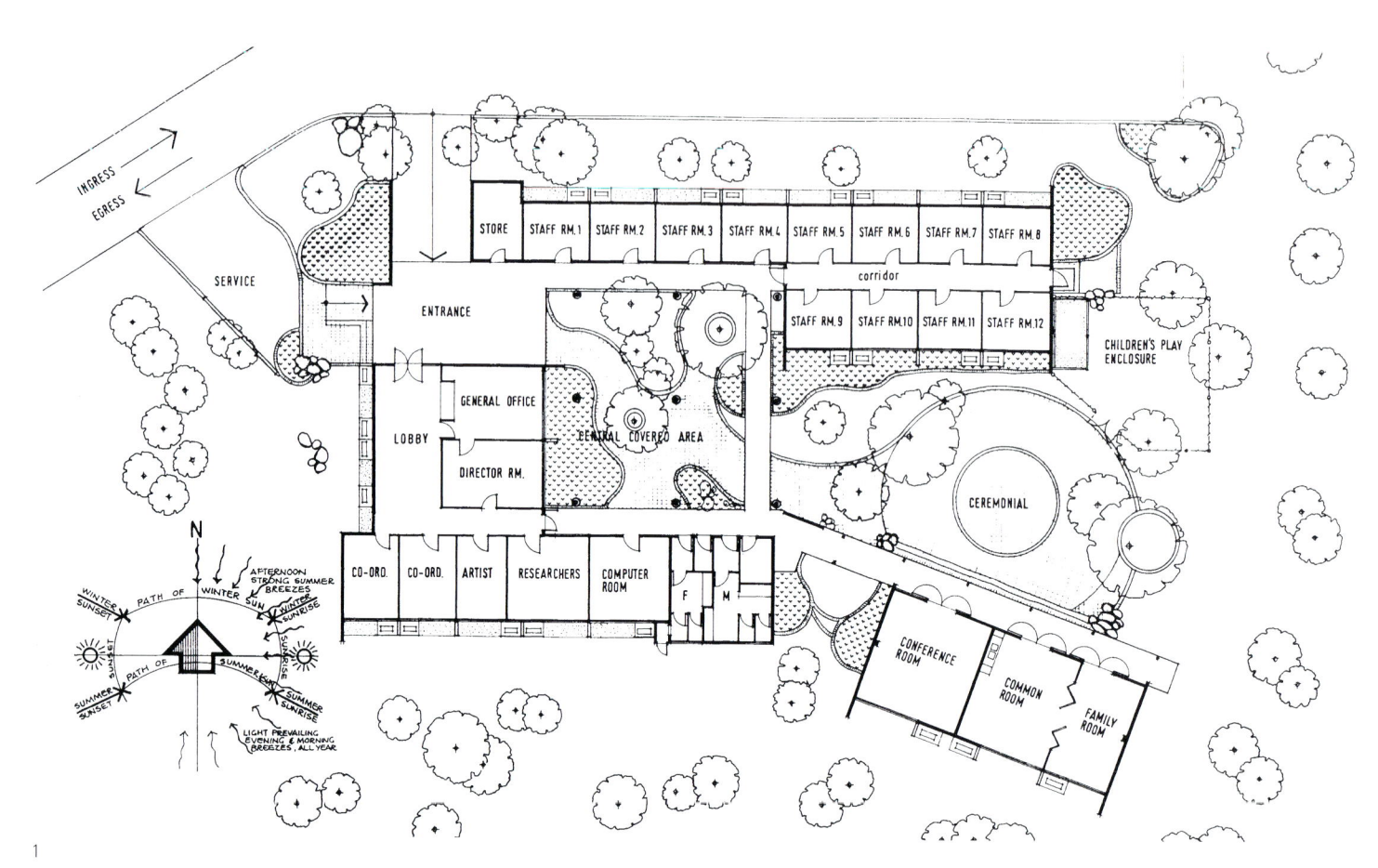

Social Sciences and Humanities Building, University of California-Davis
California, USA
Antoine Predock Architect FAIA
5   View of main stair tower
6   Courtyard level plan
7   Night view from west
8   View of stair and tower bridge from courtyard level
Photo credit: courtesy Antoine Predock Architect FAIA

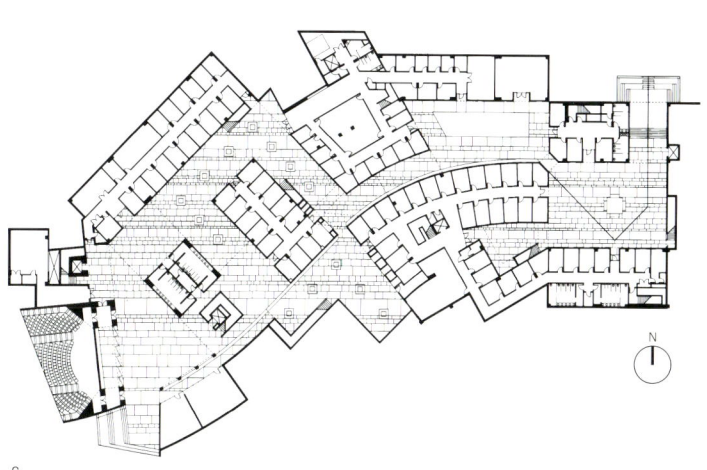

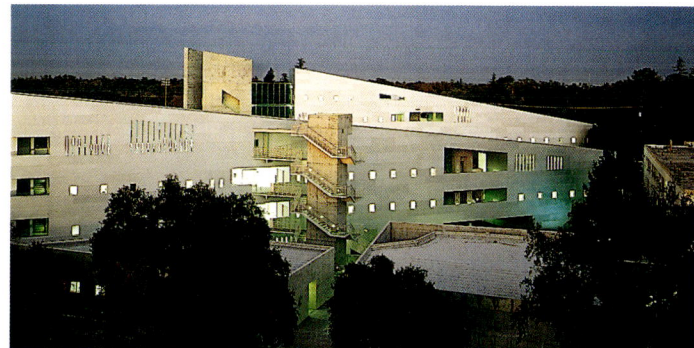

**The Learning Technology Building & Social Religious Building,
Vanderbilt University**
Nashville, Tennessee, USA
The Stubbins Associates, Inc.

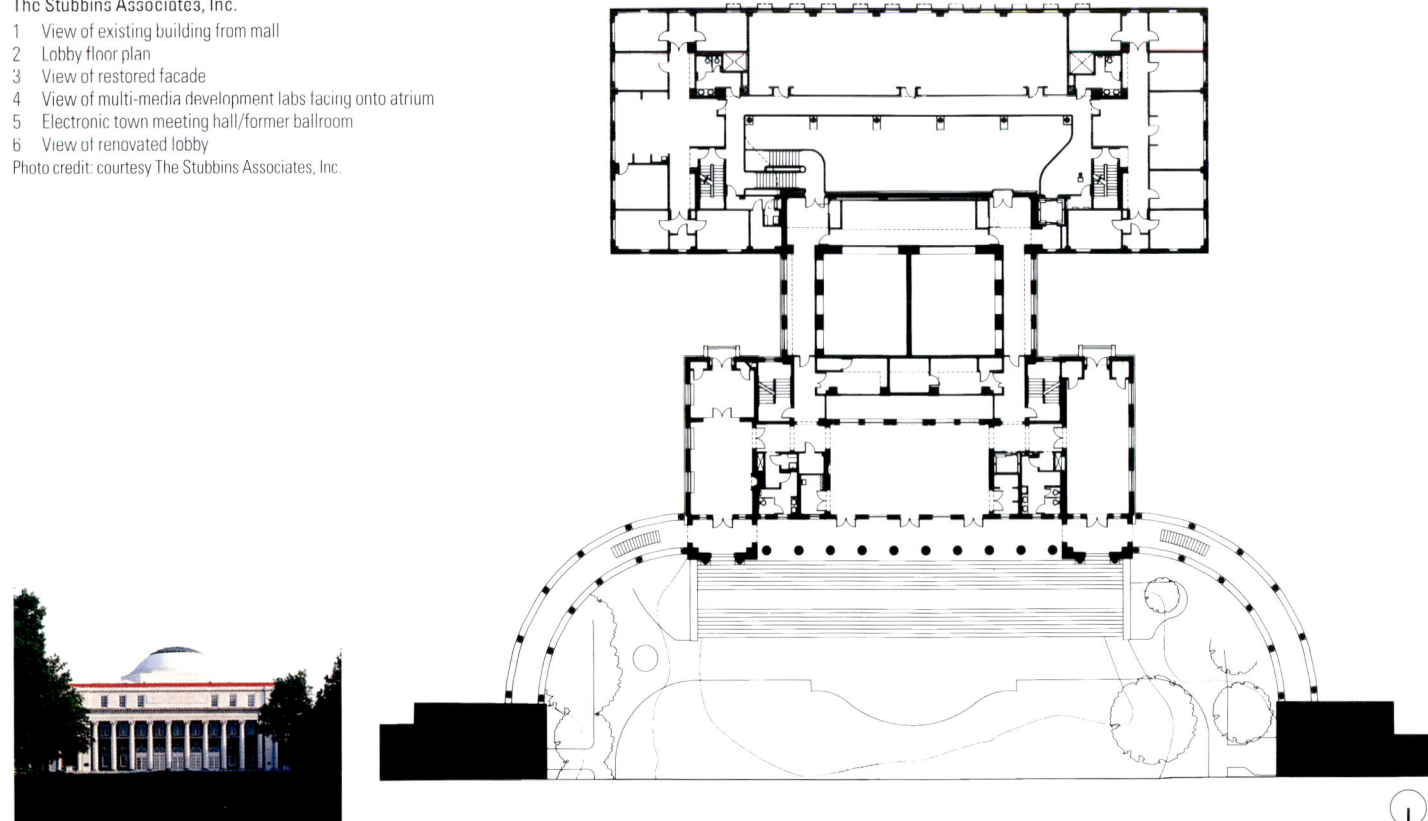

1   View of existing building from mall
2   Lobby floor plan
3   View of restored facade
4   View of multi-media development labs facing onto atrium
5   Electronic town meeting hall/former ballroom
6   View of renovated lobby

Photo credit: courtesy The Stubbins Associates, Inc.

4

5

6

Social Sciences and Computer Center, UCSD
La Jolla, California, USA
Gwathmey Siegel & Associates Architects
1 Detail of supercomputer office and entrance
2 Detail of entrance to supercomputer addition
3 View from southwest
Photo credit: Assassi Productions

Science, Industry and Business Library
New York, New York, USA
Gwathmey Siegel & Associates Architects
4 Richard B. Salomon reseach reading room
5 Electronic Information Center
Photo credit: Peter Aaron/Esto

RESEARCH READING ROOM
EXIT

4

SERVICE DESK
ELECTRONIC INFORMATION CENTER

5

Columbia University Computer Science Building
New York, New York, USA
R.M.Kliment & Frances Halsband Architects

1 Departmental courtyard
2 Conference and lounge portico
3 First floor corridor
4 First floor corridor: view to entrance hall
5 First floor corridor: view to courtyard

Photo credit: Cervin Robinson

Adult Education

1

2

3

4

Computer Science Theory Center
Cornell University
Ithaca, New York, USA
Gwathmey Siegel & Associates Architects
1 View from campus road
2 Computer classroom
3 Laboratory building from gorge
4 View from campus road
Photo credit: Timothy Hursley

Princeton University Computer Science Building
Princeton, New Jersey, USA
R.M.Kliment & Frances Halsband Architects
5 View from street
6 Main entrance from McCosh walk
7 Stair hall
8 Lecture hall
Following Page:
    Classroom lobby
Photo credit: Cervin Robinson

Adult Education 97

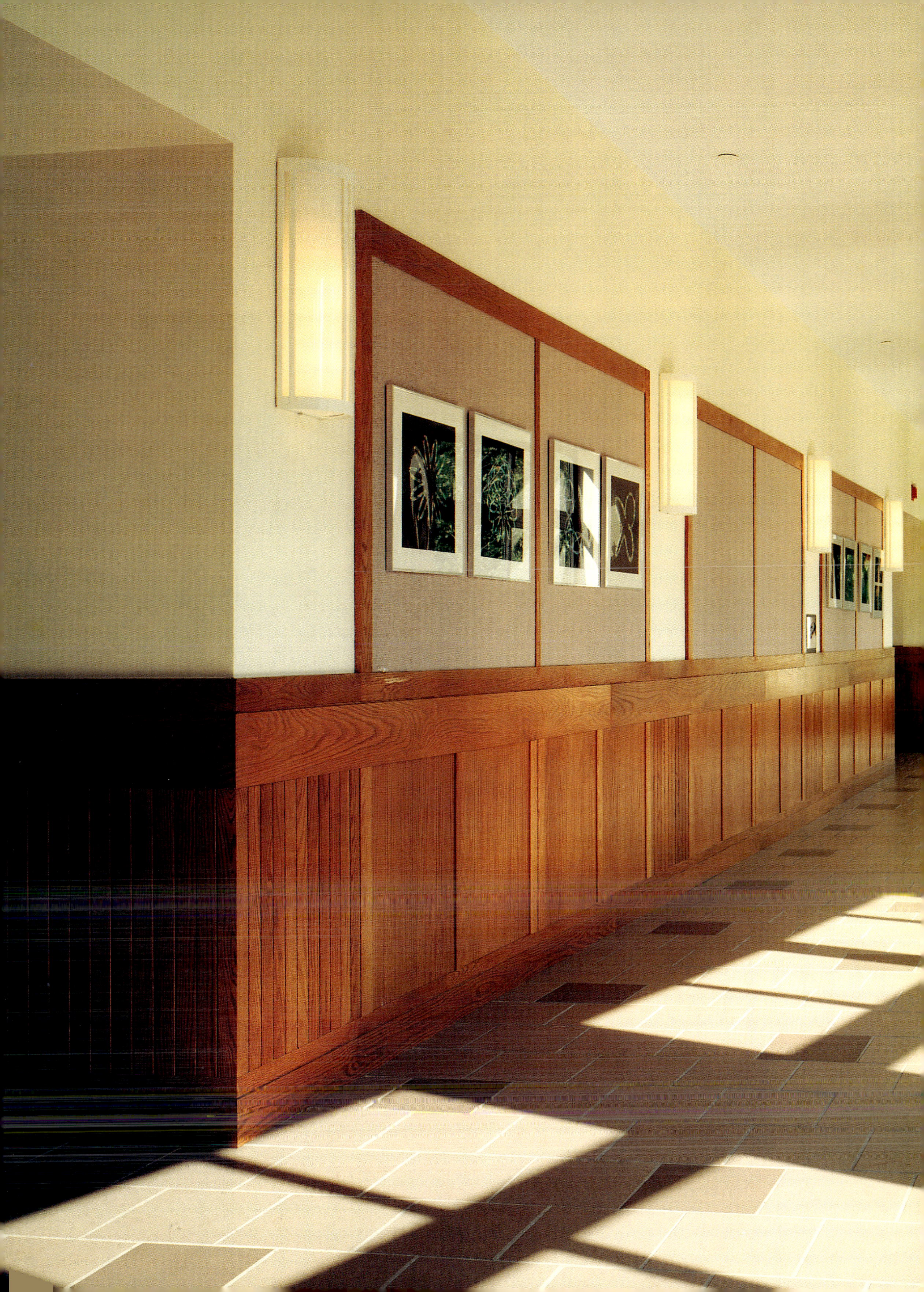

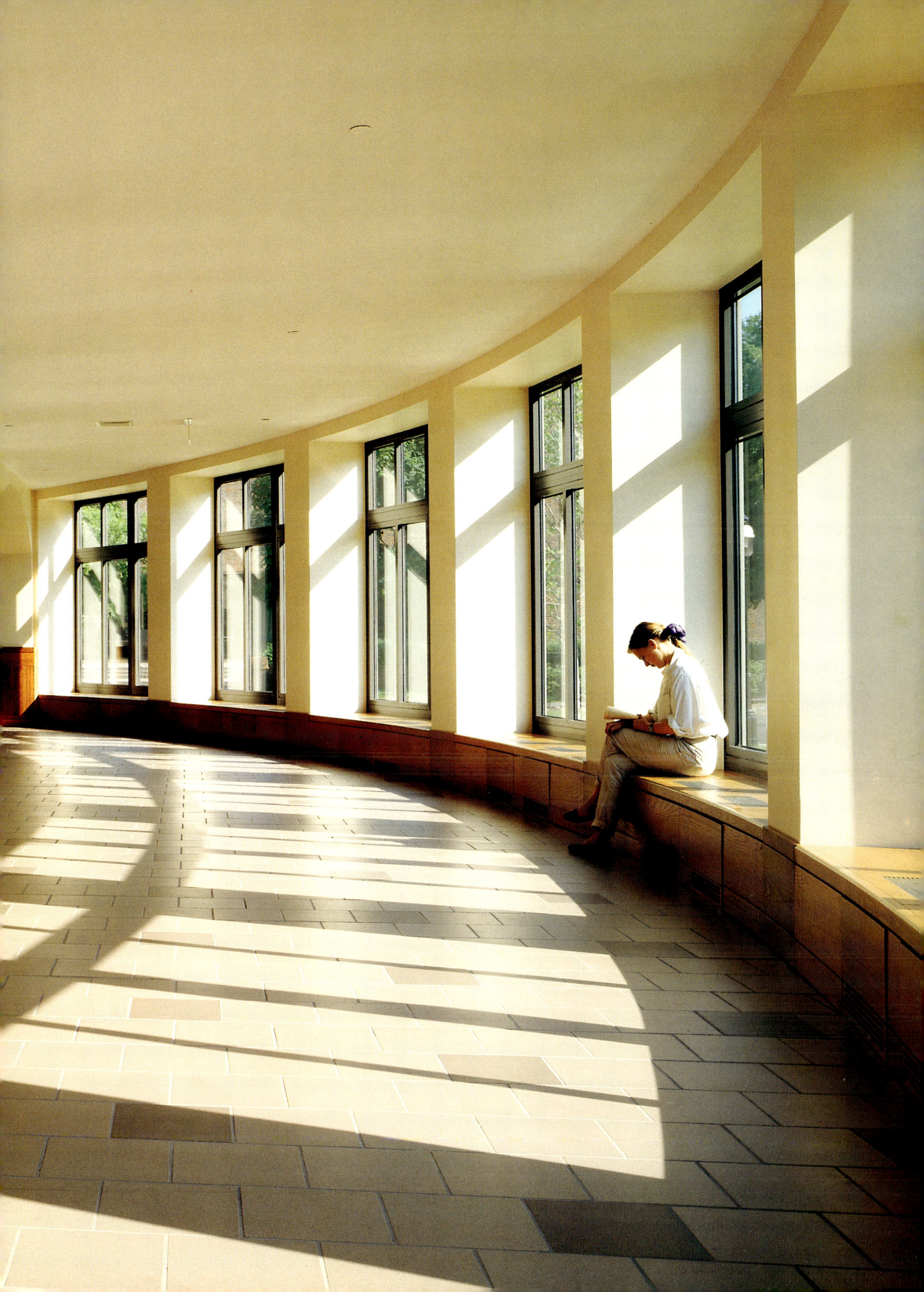

**University of Technology, Sydney
Design, Architecture and Building**
Sydney, Australia
Cox Richardson

1 Central circulation atrium, studio level
2 350 seat Guthrie Theatre
3 Studio Level 7
4 Pedestrian bridge linking the Design, Architecture and Building faculty to the main campus
5 Harris Street facade

Photo credit: Patrick Bingham-Hall

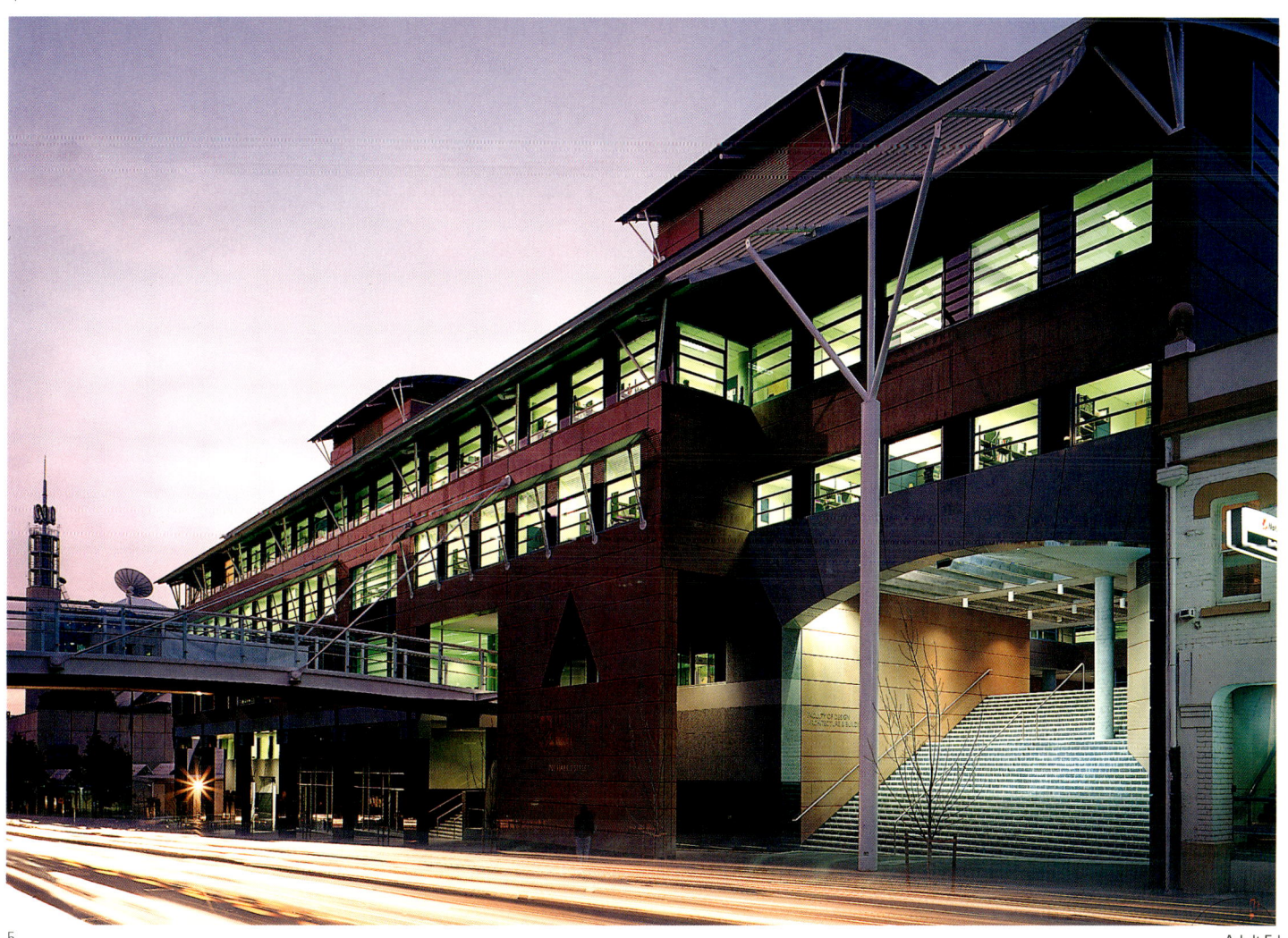

4

5

**University of Colorado,
Mathematics Building
Boulder, Colorado, USA**
Fentress Bradburn Architects
1   Campus context
2   Student plaza
3   Exterior loggia
4   Plaza exterior
5   Entry view
Photo credit: Nick Merrick/Hedrich Blessing,
Thorney Lieberman

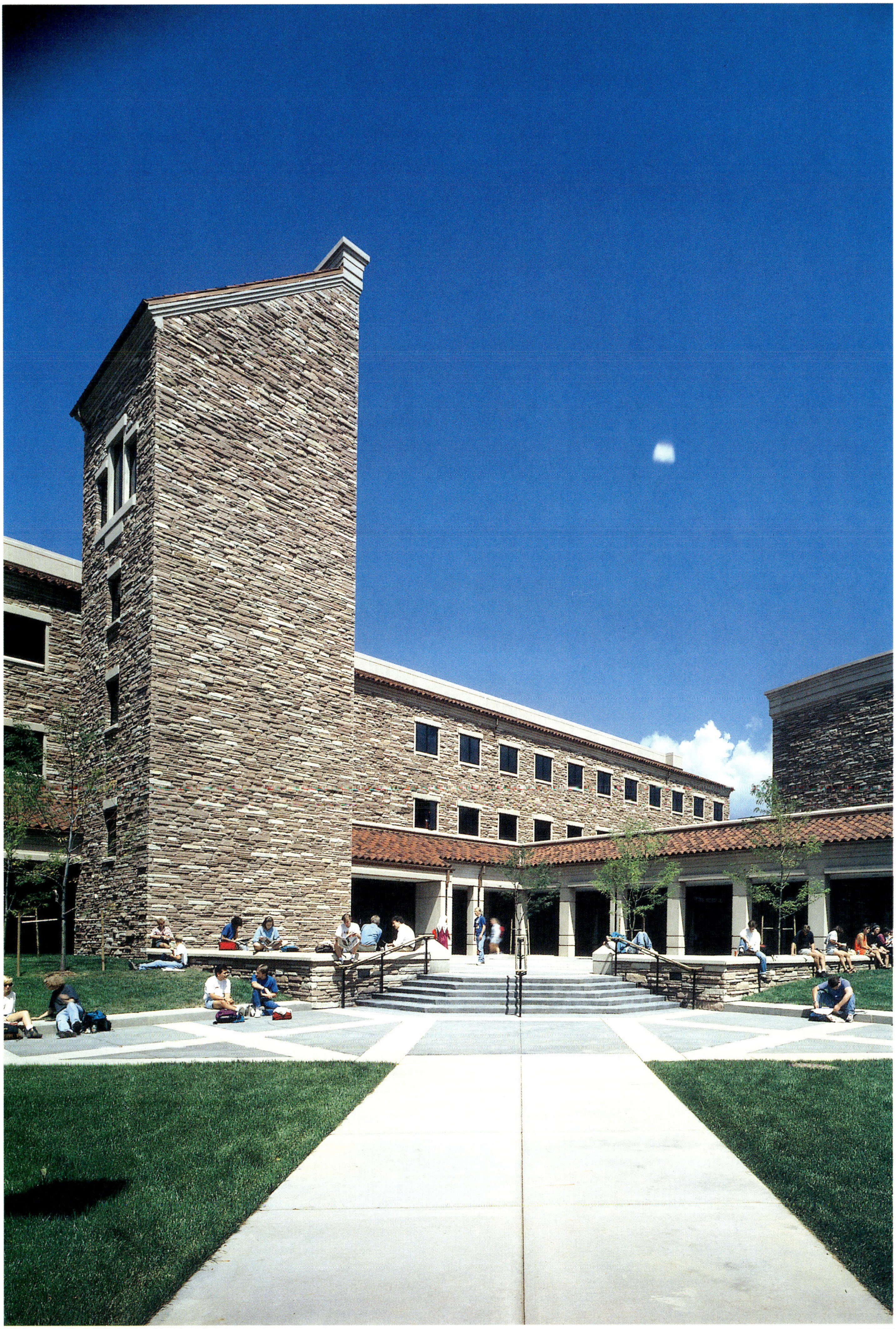

5

1

2

University of Cincinnati, Engineering Research Center
Cincinnati, Ohio, USA
Michael Graves Architect

1 Second level of entrance stairhall
2 Lecture hall
3 View of entrance facade from south
4 Copper roof detail
5 View from northwest
Photo credit: Steven Brooke

C.N.R. Research Facility
Bologna, Italy
Enzo Zacchiroli Architetto
1&2 Inside view of library
3 Conforonco hall in service management centre
4 View of inside courtyard of service management centre
5 Inside stairbody in the service management centre hall
6 View of stairbody in institute
7 Library
Photo credits: Stefano Parisini (1—3,5), Antonio Cesari (4,6,7)

Magee-Womens Hospital, Education Centre at Womancare Oakland
Pittsburgh, Pennsylvania, USA
Tsoi/Kobus & Associates Architects
8 Atrium
9 Conference centre
10 Auditorium
Photo credit: Scott McDonald/Hedrich Blessing

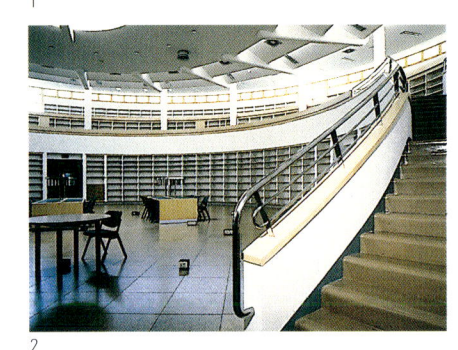

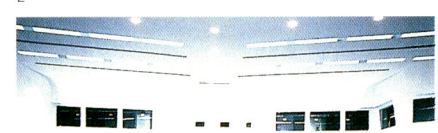

Adult Education

1
2
3 4

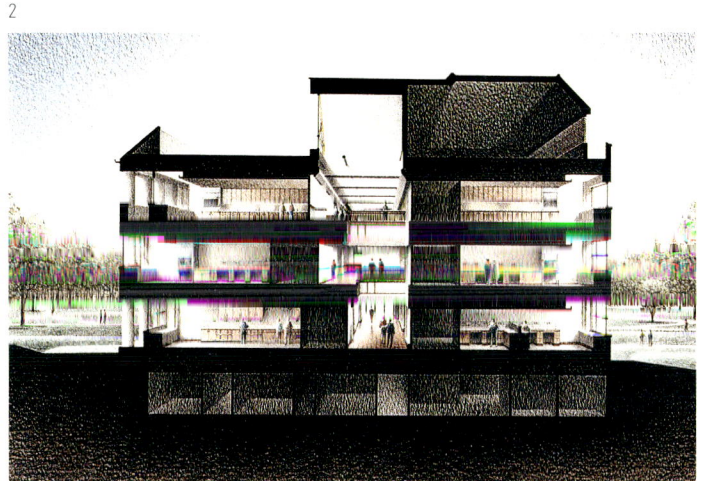

**Hulings Hall Biological Sciences Building,
Carleton College
Northfield, Minnesota, USA**
The Stubbins Associates, Inc.
1 The sloping mechanical room roof and articulated facade reduce the scale of the building on the courtyard
2 Front view from quadrangle
3 The new building completes the enclosure of the campus green and enhances the spatial organisation of the campus
4 Pendant-mounted lighting fixtures reduce energy consumption and provide an enhanced visual environment

Photo credit: courtesy The Stubbins Associates, Inc.

**Biological Sciences Learning Center and
Jules F. Knapp Medical Research Center,
University of Chicago
Chicago, Illinois, USA**
The Stubbins Associates, Inc.
5 The design responds to the established campus architecture
6 Typical teaching laboratory
7 Each greenhouse is environmentally sealed to protect the integrity of the research being conducted

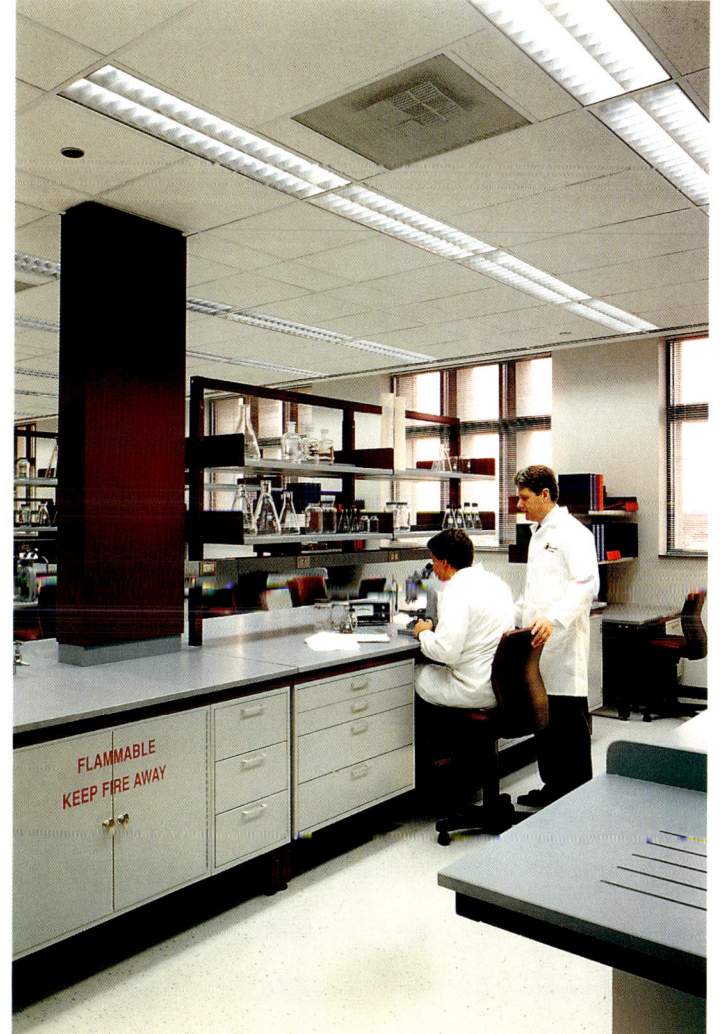

Photo credit: courtesy The Stubbins Associates, Inc.

Arts and Sciences Building, Richard Stockton College of New Jersey
Pomona, New Jersey, USA
Michael Graves Architect

1   Site and ground floor plan
2   Entrance facade
3   Second floor lounge
4   South facade along college walk
Opposite:
    Courtyard entrance
Photo credit: Marek Bulaj

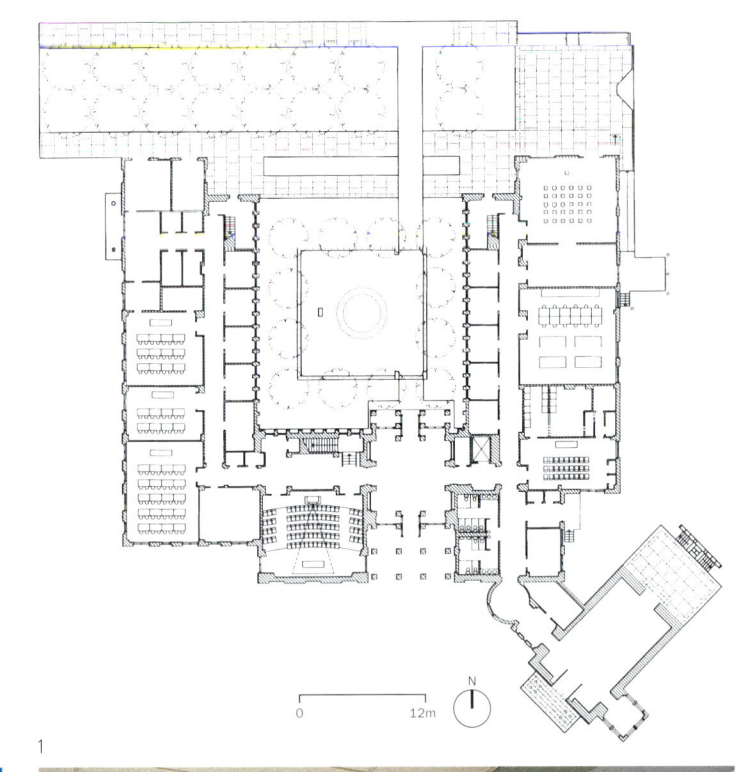

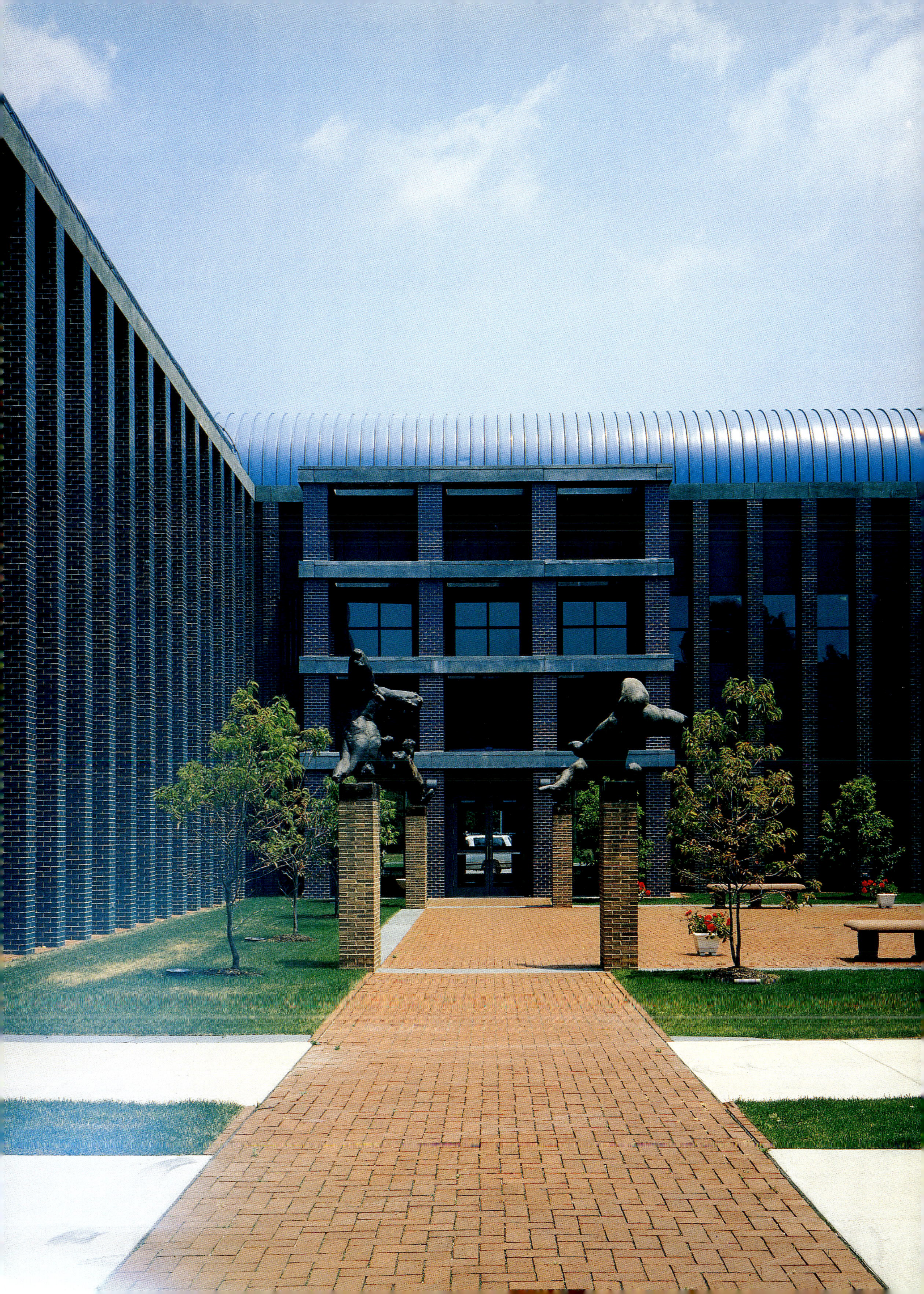

**Harvard Medical School,
Medical Education Center**
Boston, Massachusetts, USA
Ellenzweig Associates, Inc.
1 First floor plan
2 Main entrance
3 View from northeast, with adjacent existing building
4 Redesigned amphitheatre
5 Skylit atrium, with existing walls of original building
Photo credit: Steve Rosenthal

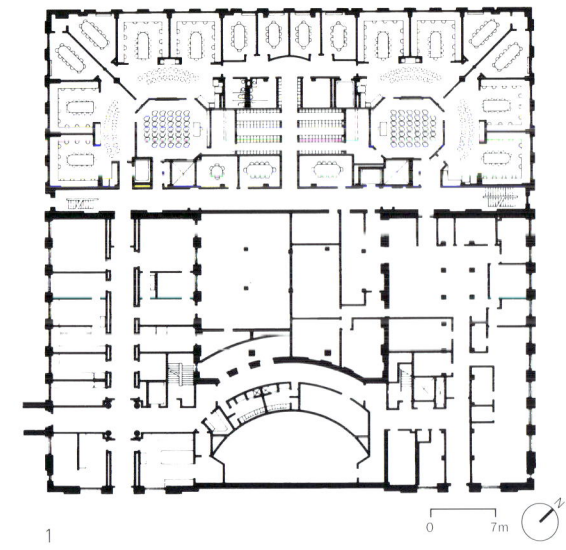

4

5

Adult Education 113

Harvard Medical School, Medical Education Center
Boston, Massachusetts, USA
Ellenzweig Associates, Inc.
6 Case study classroom
Photo credit: Steve Rosenthal

Harvard Medical School
Boston, Massachusetts, USA
Tsoi/Kobus & Associates Architects
7 Pathology and microbiology building conference room
8 Biochemistry and physiology building auditorium
9 Biochemistry and physiology building break-out area
10 Administration building atrium
Photo credit: Steve Rosenthal (7), Sam Sweezy (8,9), David Hewitt & Anne Garrison (10)

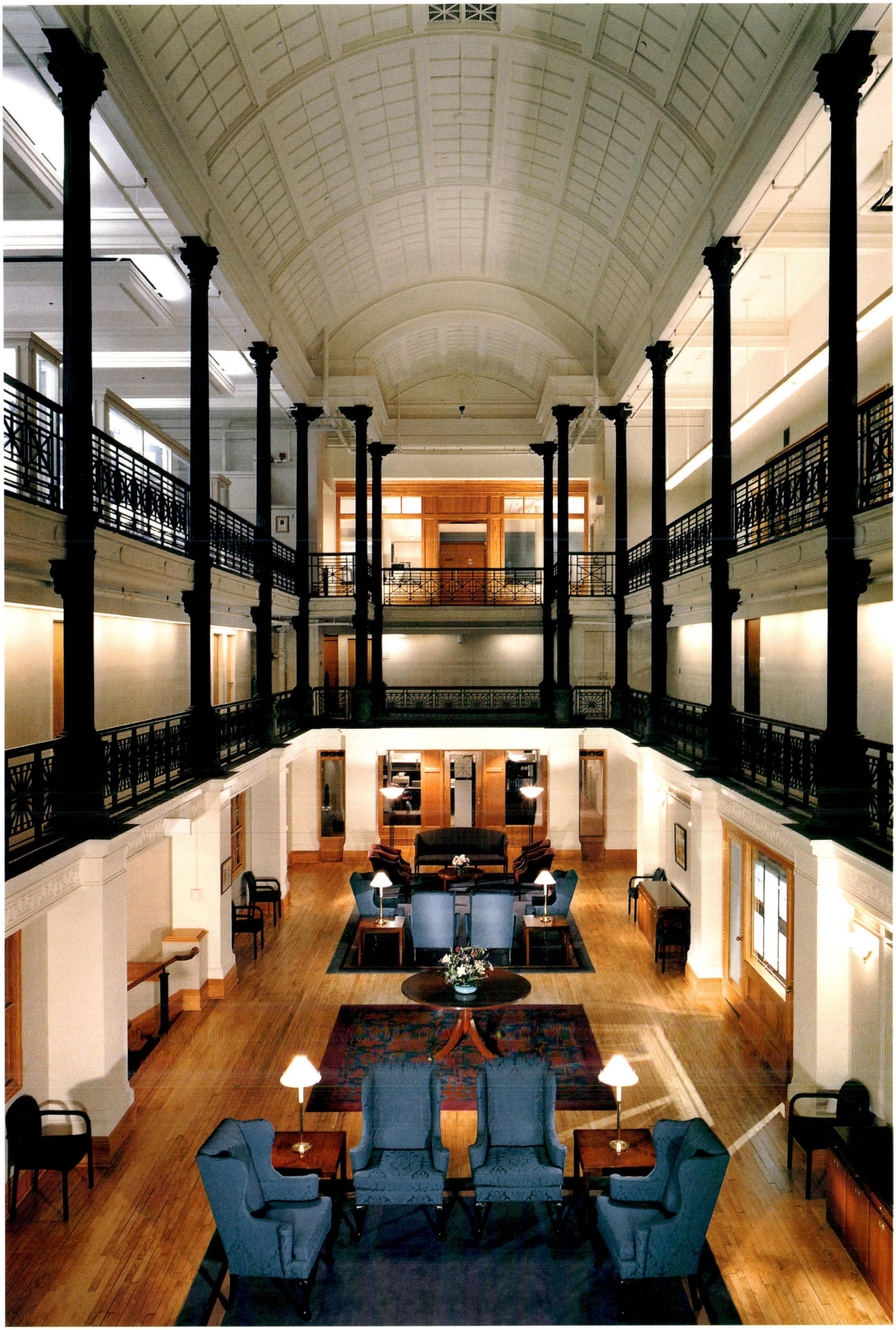

10

College of Agriculture and Life Sciences
Cornell University
Ithaca, New York, USA
Gwathmey Siegel & Associates Architects
1   Entry gate from Bailey Plaza
2   Entry to academic building from Tower Road
3   600-seat auditorium
4   Circulation gallery in academic building
Opposite:
    Landscape architecture studio
Photo credit: Jeff Goldberg/Esto (1,3,4), Timothy Hursley (2, opposite)

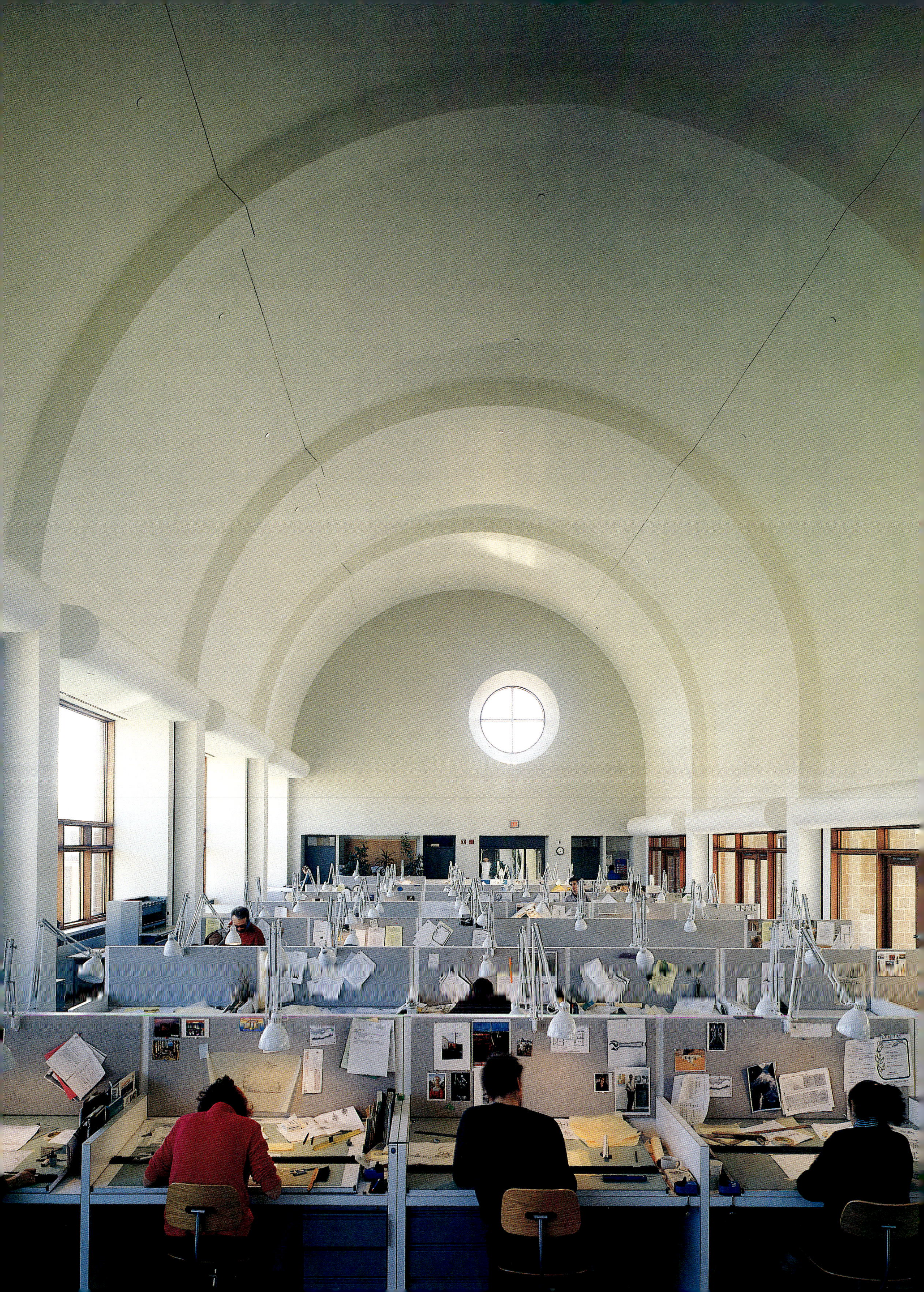

Earth Sciences Centre
University of Toronto, Ontario, Canada
A.J. Diamond, Donald Schmitt and
Company with Dregman & Hamann
1   Stair and carriageway at laboratory block
2   North courtyard and colonnade
3   View into south courtyard with library on left
4   Departmental stair
Photo credit: Steven Evans

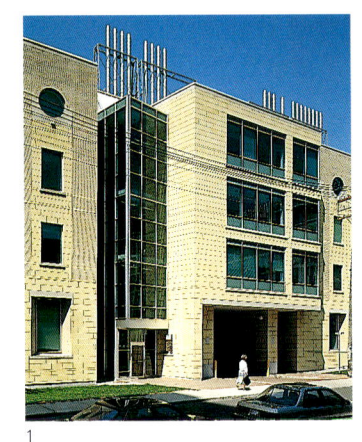

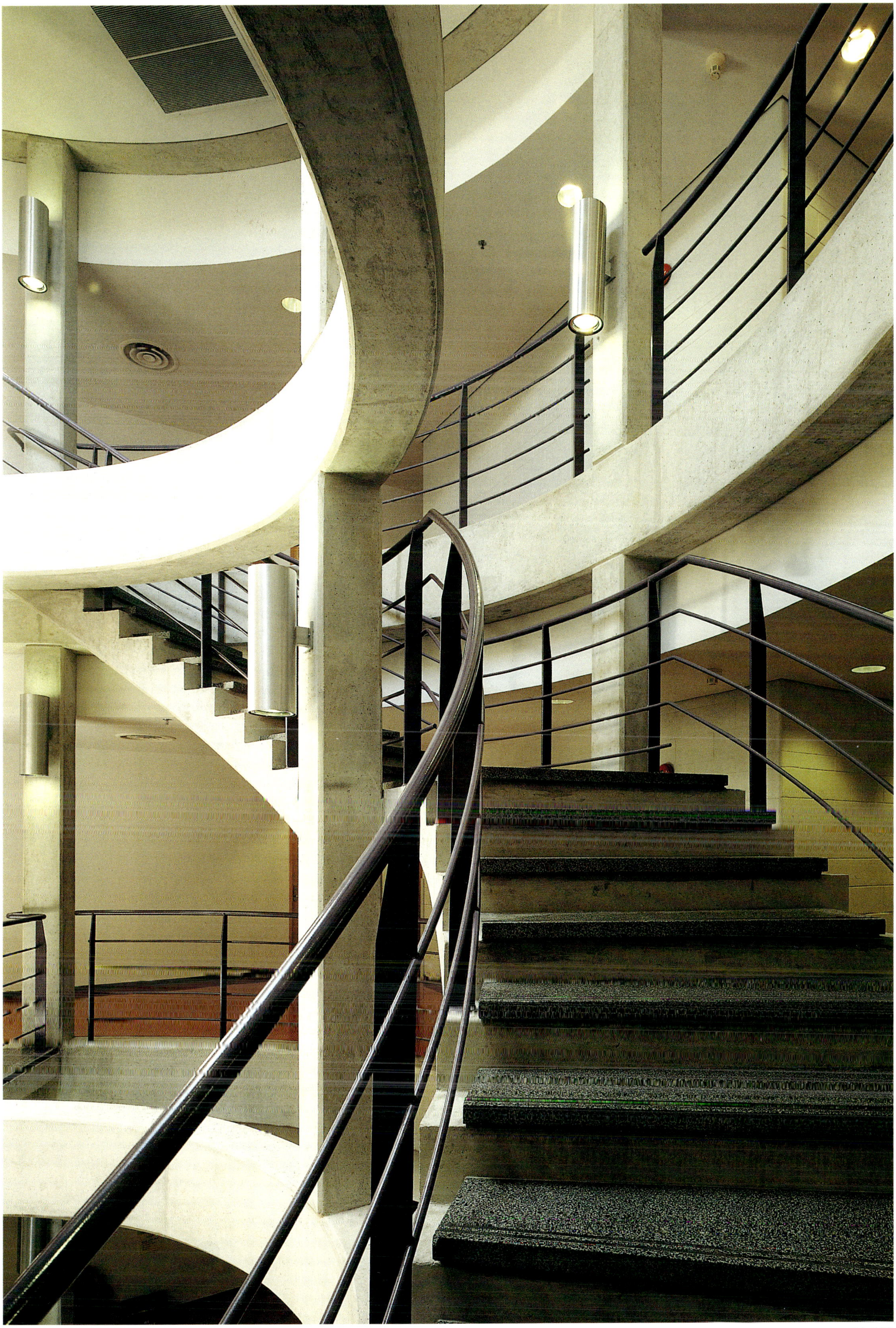

4

The University of Wisconsin
Instructional Greenhouses
Wisconsin, USA
Flad & Associates

1 Floor plan
2 Entryway polycarbonate canopy and Glulam trees cover visitors
3 The facility marches gracefully before plant sciences
4 Entrance corridor provides interior and exterior plantscape views
5 Glazing system clads conservatory superstructure
6 Conservatory features an automatic misting/shade feature

Photo credit: Steve Hall/Hedrich Blessing

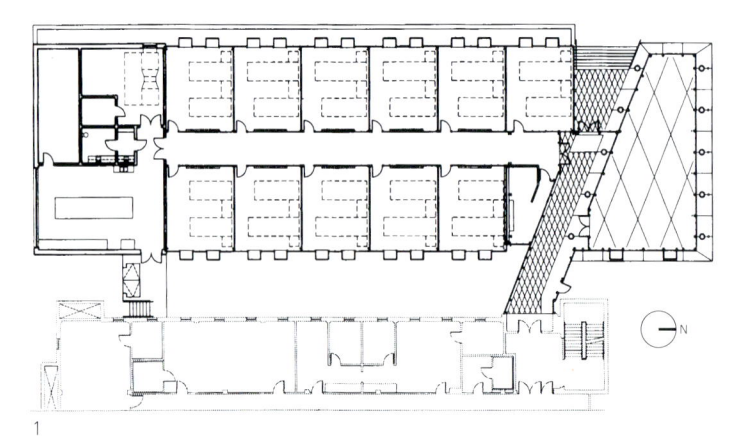

4

5

6

Adult Education 121

SUNY at Albany's Center for Environmental Sciences & Technology Management
Albany, New York, USA
Cannon

1 Labs are either computer, wet or dry, but capable of any adaptation
2 Showcase of technology, the Center comprises one of the largest building-integrated photovaltaic assemblies in the USA
3 Skylit lobby is main public space
4 In sweeping form, the Center culminates in a 115-foot high communication tower, both a functional and symbolic focal point
5 CESTM has three components: research labs, business incubator and entry rotunda

Photo credit: Esto Photography

Cambridge University Law Faculty
Cambridge, UK
Foster and Partners

6 Interior

Photo credit: courtesy Foster and Partners

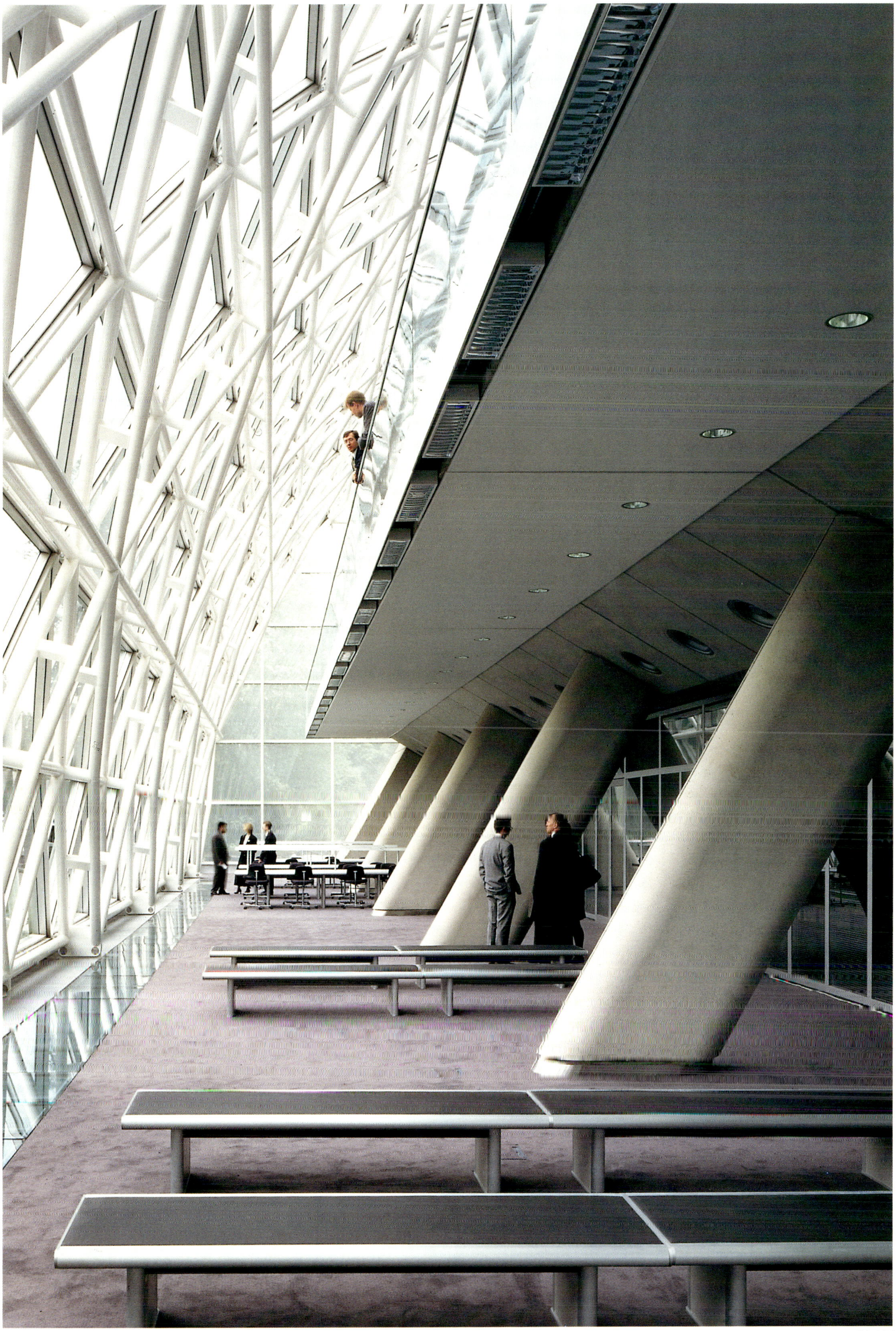

6

**Cambridge University Law Faculty
Cambridge, UK**
Foster and Partners
7 Ground floor plan
8 Roof detail at entrance canopy
9 Curved glass wall
10 Exterior at night
11 Library shelving designed by Foster and
   Partners
12 Interior of atrium
13 Interior
Photo credit: courtesy Foster and Partners

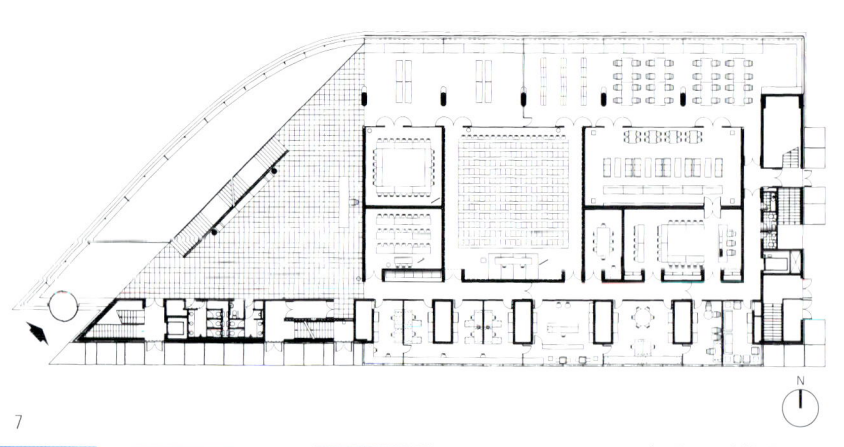

11

12

13

1

2

3

Clement House, London School of Economics
London, UK
Shepheard Epstein Hunter
1   Clement House from Aldwych, London
2   New seven storey staircase inserted against a party wall
3   Old banking hall converted to main lecture theatre
4   Third floor café overlooking the River Thames
Photo credit: courtesy Shepheard Epstein Hunter

**MNBA Hall and Purnell Hall Renovation,
University of Delaware**
Newark, Delaware, USA
The Stubbins Associates, Inc.
1   View of overall building
2   Typical classroom
3   Atrium view with custom light fixture
4   Stairway details
5   Office alcove area
Photo credit: courtesy The Stubbins Associates, Inc.

Adult Education

Student Affairs and Administrative Services Building
University of California-Santa Barbara,
California, USA
Antoine Predock Architect FAIA
1   View from Cheadle Courtyard to Student Affairs, looking west
Photo credit: courtesy Antoine Predock Architect FAIA

Adult Education 131

Student Affairs and Administrative Services Building
University of California-Santa Barbara, California, USA
Antoine Predock Architect FAIA
2 View from west towards Visitor Center entrance
3 View looking south to Visitor Center
4 Detail of grand stairway
5 Southern entry at bike path
Photo credit: courtesy Antoine Predock Architect FAIA

UCLA Northwest Campus Housing & Commons Buildings
Los Angeles, California, USA
Barton Myers Associates, Inc.
6 Interior courtyard of Student Housing
Photo credit: Tim Griffith

5

6

7

8

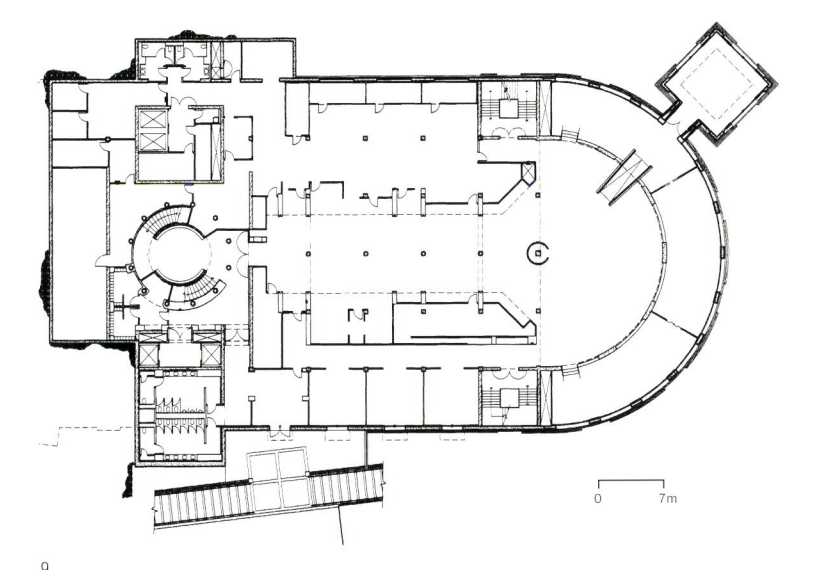

UCLA Northwest Campus Housing & Commons Buildings
Los Angeles, California, USA
Barton Myers Associates, Inc.

7 Entry tower and plaza facade of Commons Building
8 Large porch and terrace off main conference room
9 Ground floor plan
10 View to lower floor access at spiral stair
11 Main ceiling appears to float over spiral stair
12 Sitting area/ terrazzo medallion at base of main stair

Photo credit: Tim Griffith

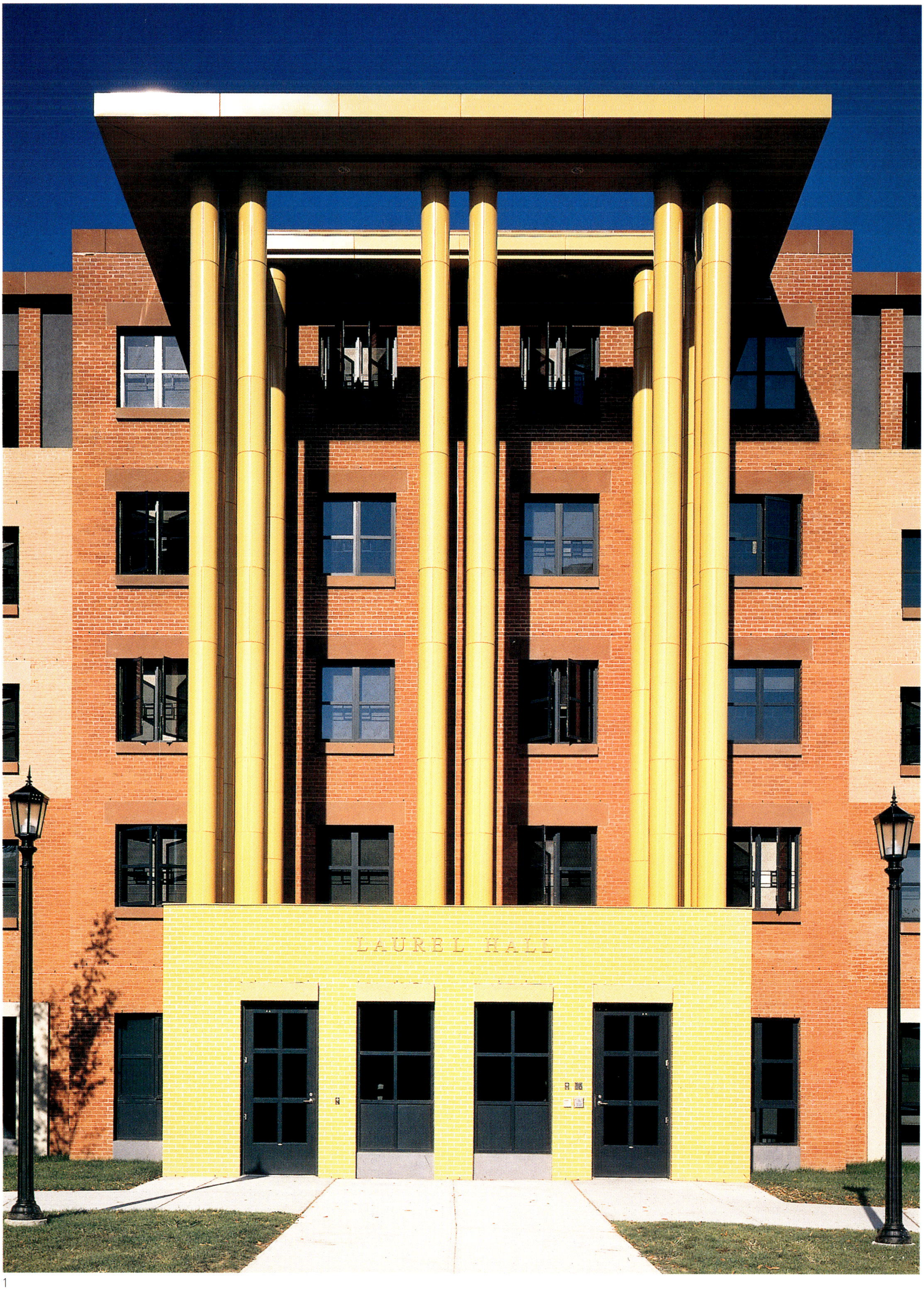

1

3

**New Residence Hall (Laurel Hall),
New Jersey Institute of Technology
Newark, New Jersey, USA**
Michael Graves Architect
1–3   Main entrance
Photo credit: Robert Faulkner

**York University Student Centre, York University
Toronto, Ontario, Canada**
A.J. Diamond, Donald Schmitt and Company
4   Student pub
Photo credit: Steven Evans

York University Student Centre, York University
Toronto, Ontario, Canada
A.J. Diamond, Donald Schmitt and Company
5   Stairs at upper floors of student offices
6   Student pub
7   Public circulation
Photo credit: Steven Evans

Adult Education 139

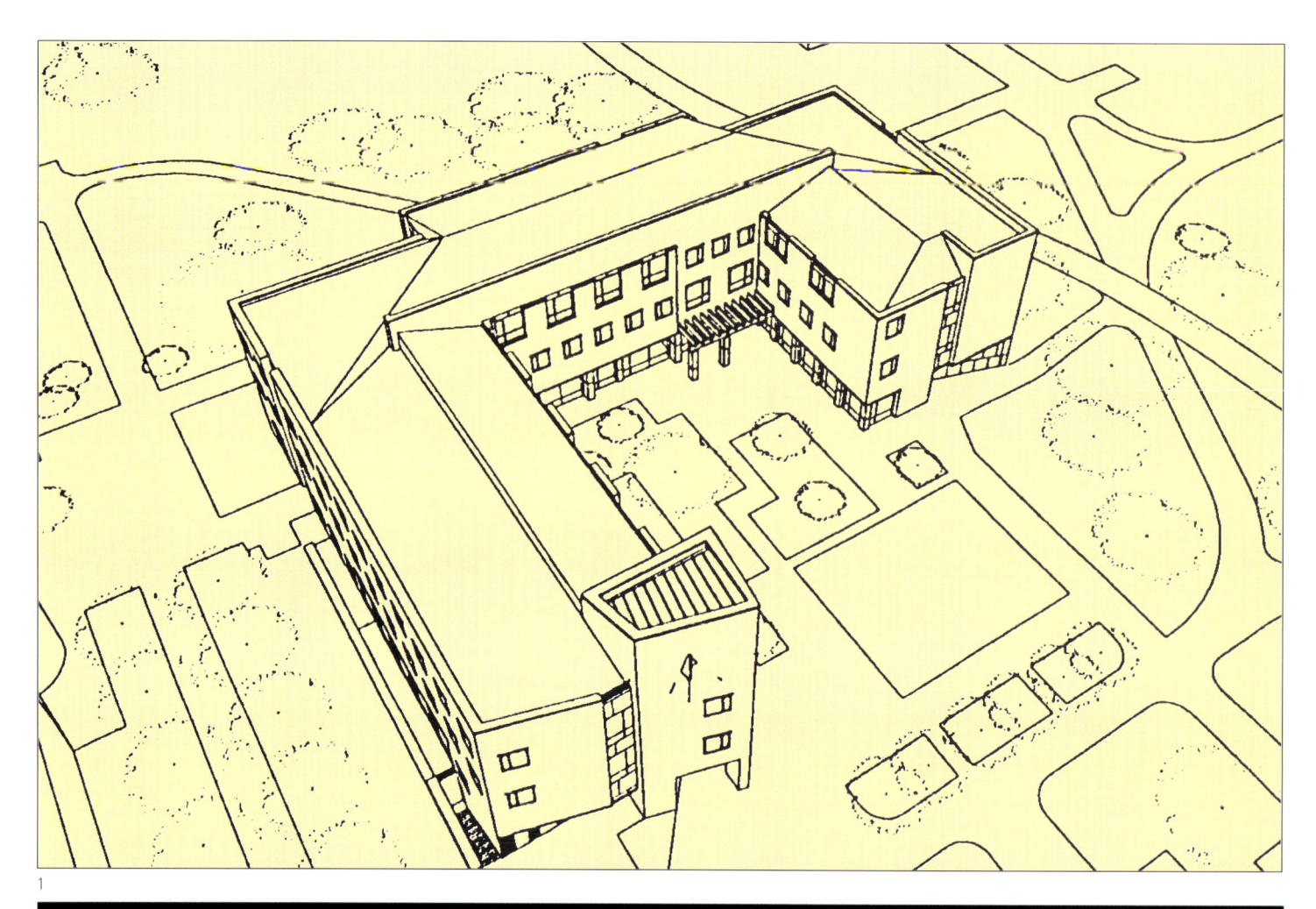

1

2

Swarthmore College, Kohlberg Hall
Swarthmore, Pennsylvania, USA
Margaret Helfand Architects

1. Axonometric perspective
2. View looking north to courtyard from Parrish Hall
3. View of commons at dusk
4. Interior view of commons and coffee bar
5. View looking east of tower showing sundial
6. Interior view of tower seminar room

Photo credit: courtesy Margaret Helfand Architects

University of Rochester
Rochester, Minnesota, USA
The Stubbins Associates, Inc.
1   Overall building with entry rotunda
2   Entry rotunda at dusk
3   Informal lounge space overlooking entry rotunda
4   Detail of cable system supporting glass structure in entry rotunda
Opposite:
    Entry rotunda featuring glass sculpture by Ed Carpenter
Photo credit: courtesy The Stubbins Associates, Inc.

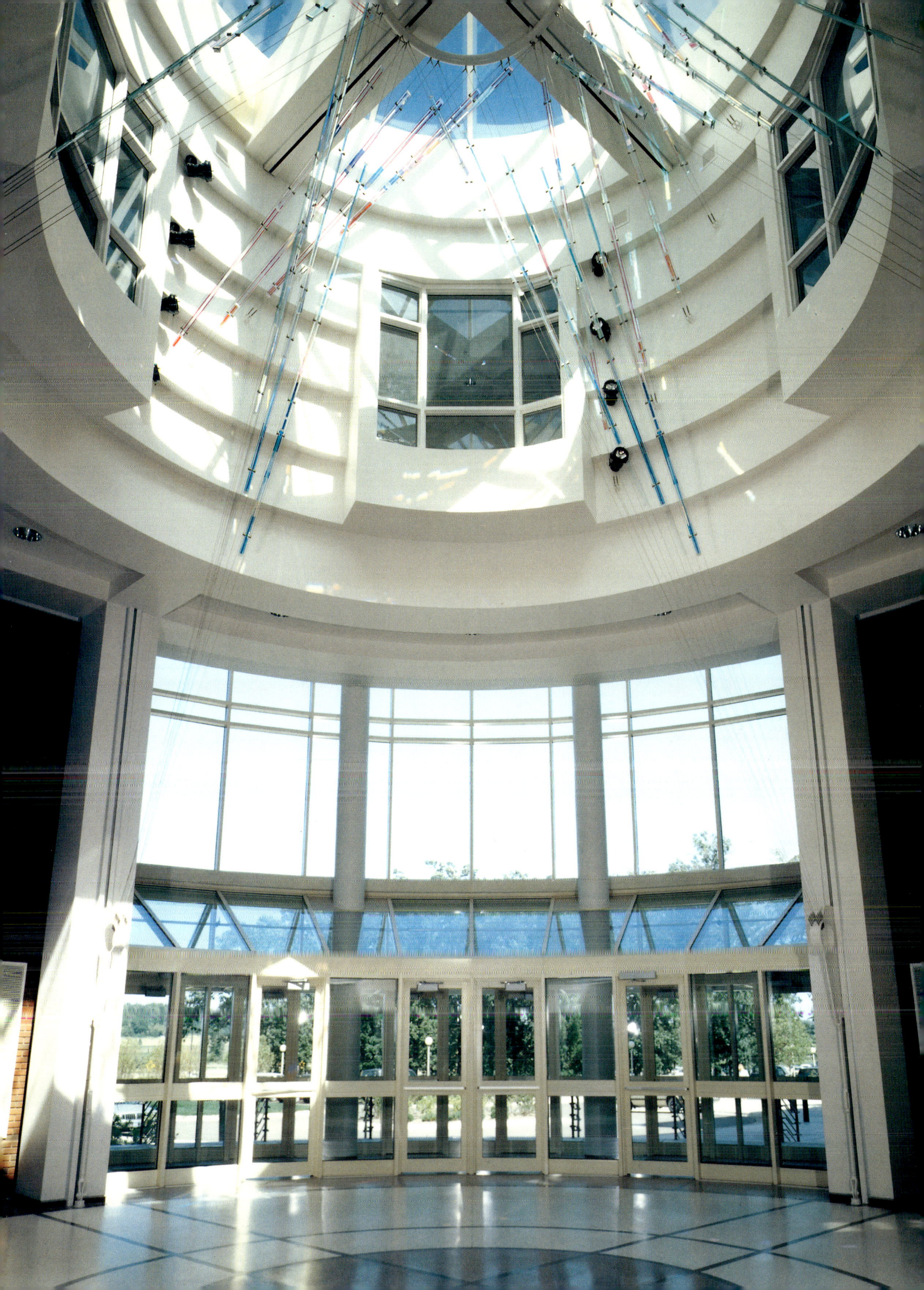

**Spencer T. Olin Hall, Student Union,
Washington University School of Medicine**
St. Louis, Missouri, USA
Mackey Mitchell Associates

1   Sculptural limestone seating area with view toward dining area
2   Detail of light monitor (conical, drywall)
3   Connecting ramp from cafeteria to lounge
4   View of informal lounge area
Photo credit: Alise O'Brien

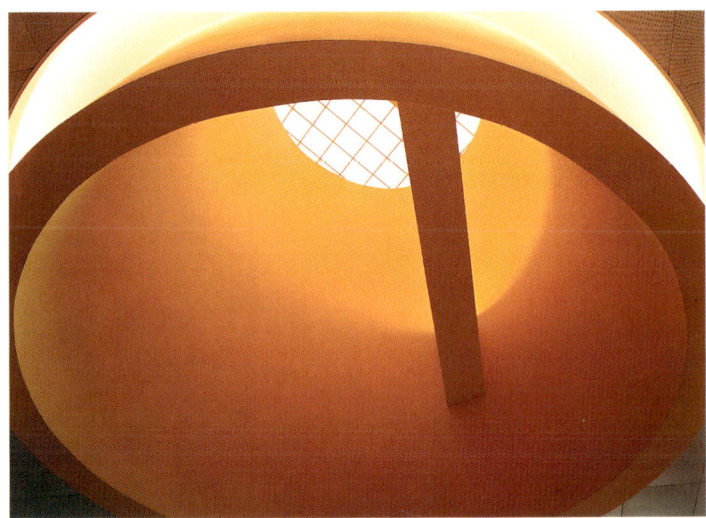

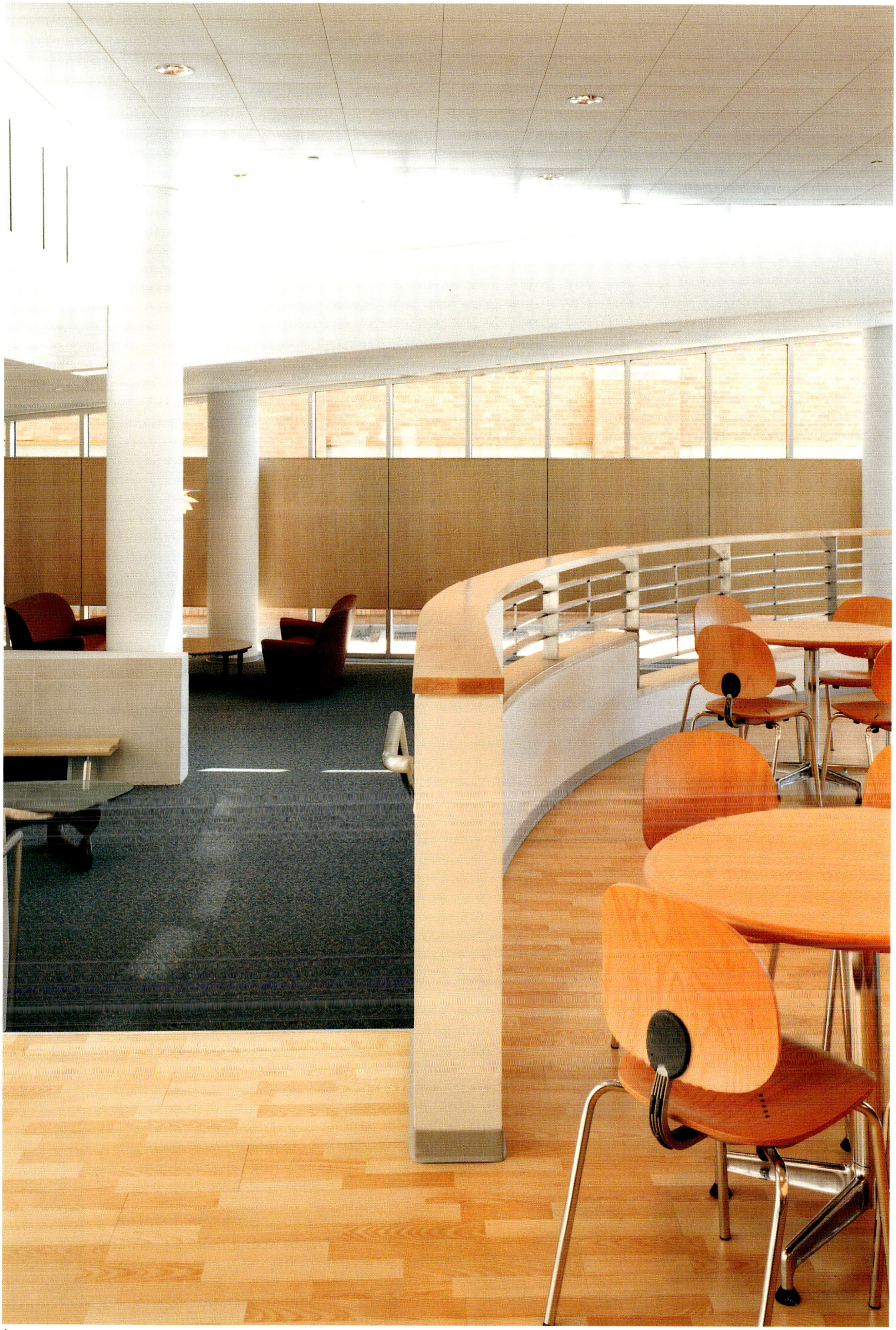

4

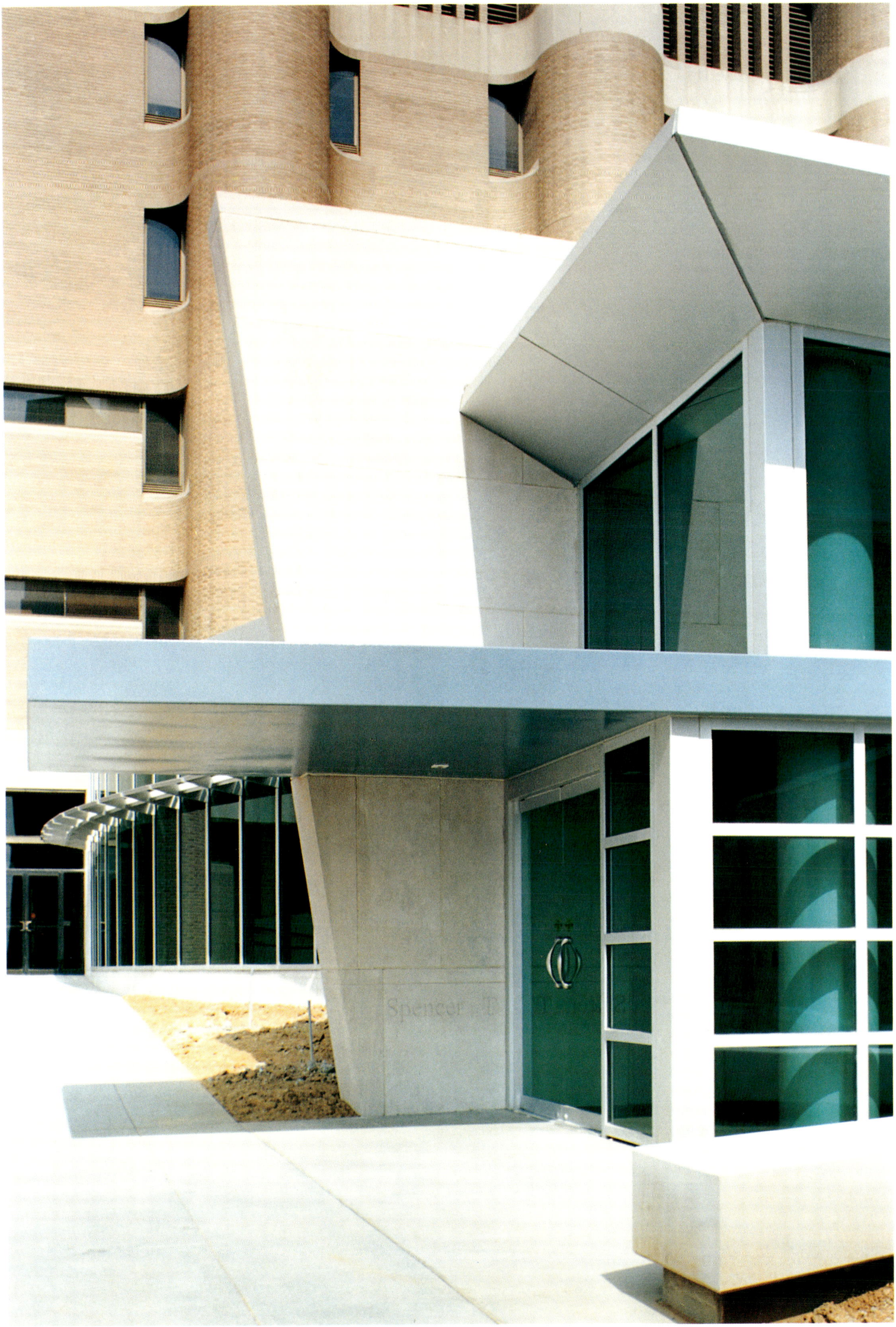

Spencer T. Olin Hall, Student Union,
Washington University School of Medicine
St. Louis, Missouri, USA
Mackey Mitchell Associates
5   Detail of new main entry to Spencer T. Olin Hall
Photo credit: Alise O'Brien

David Saul Smith Union, Bowdoin College
Brunswick, Maine, USA
Hardy Holzman Pfeiffer Associates
6   Bright lounge features ramp connecting various elements and the "Bowdoin Sun" college seal in linoleum
Photo credit: Brian Vanden Brink

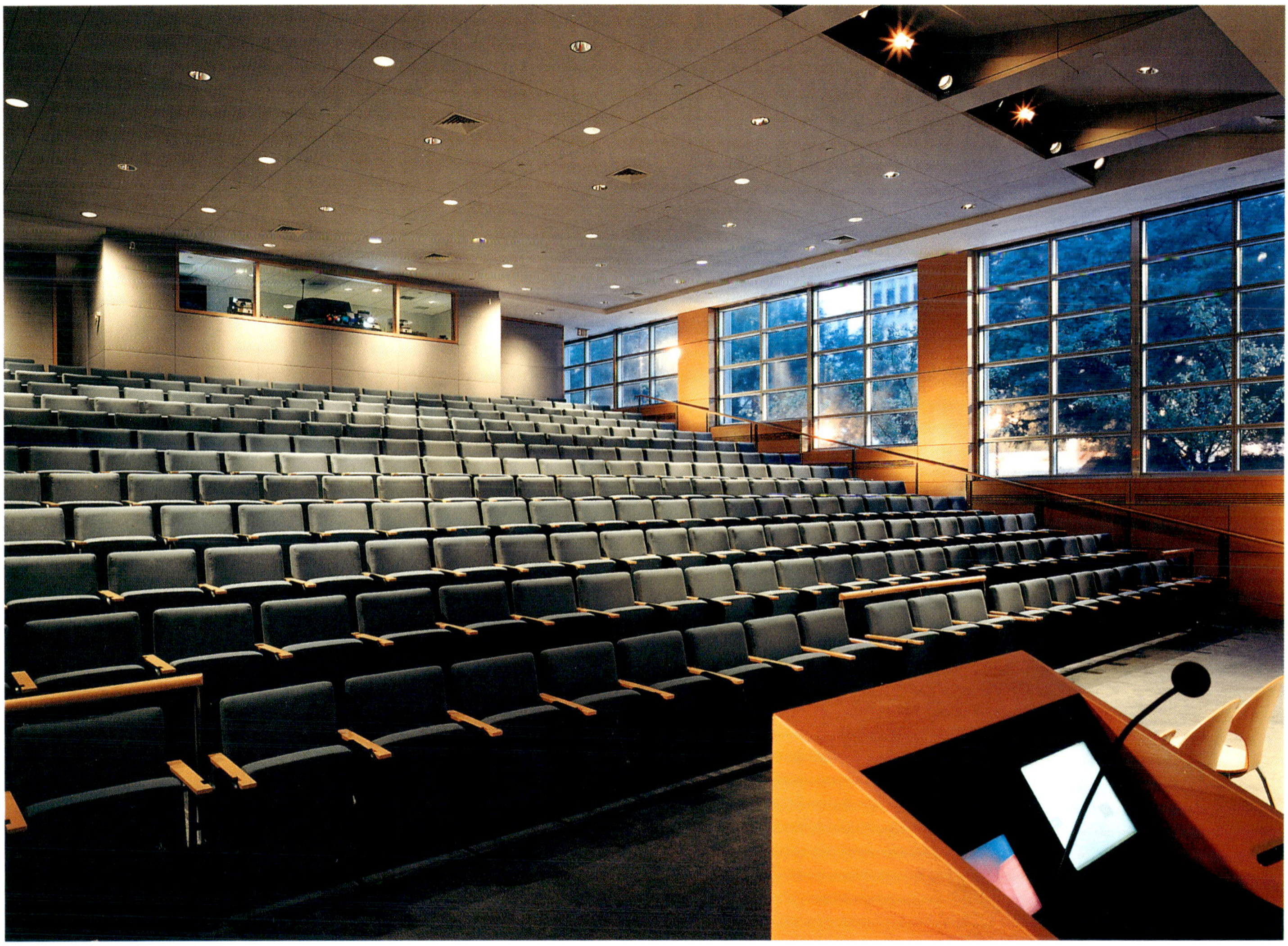
1

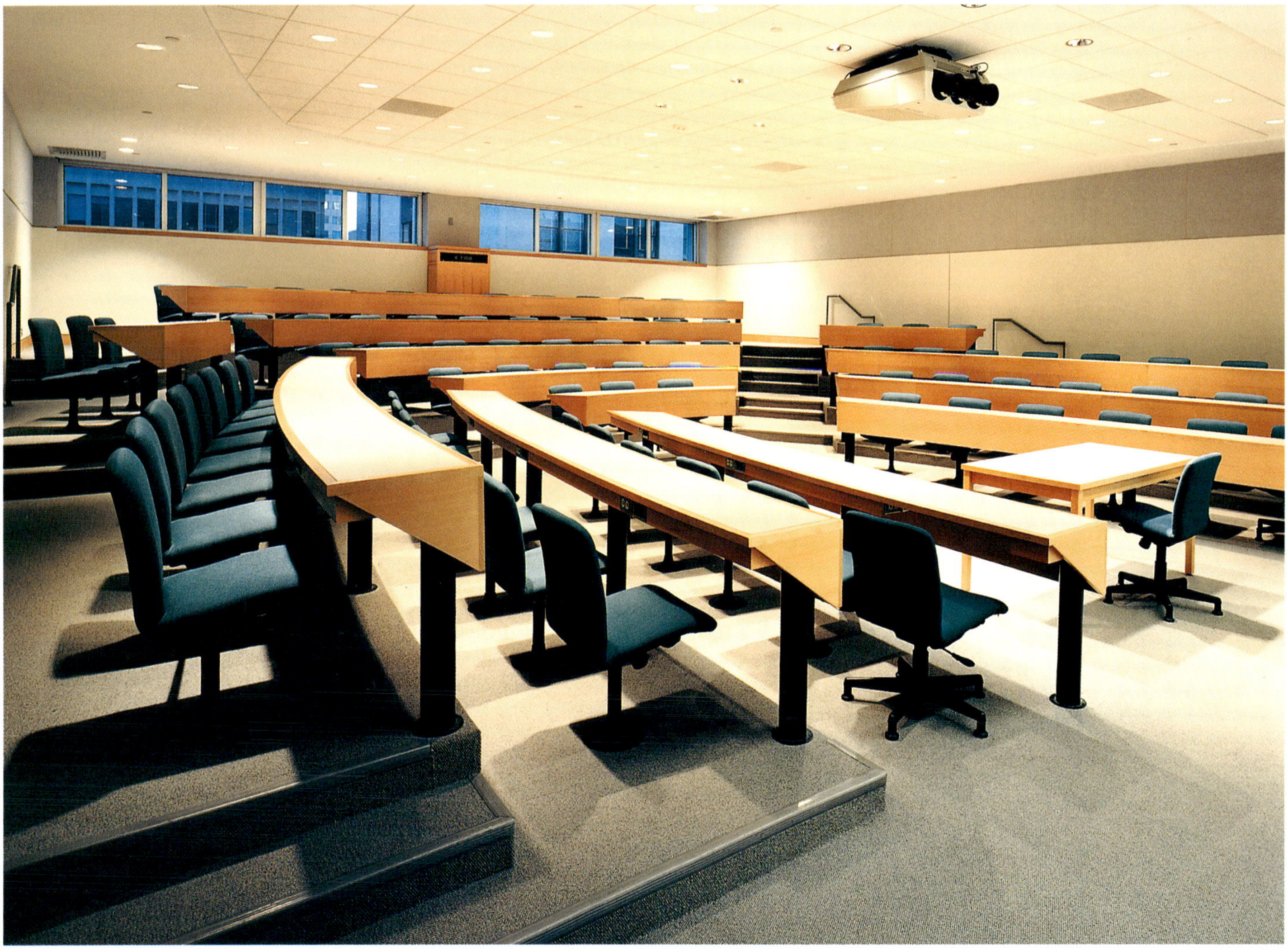
2

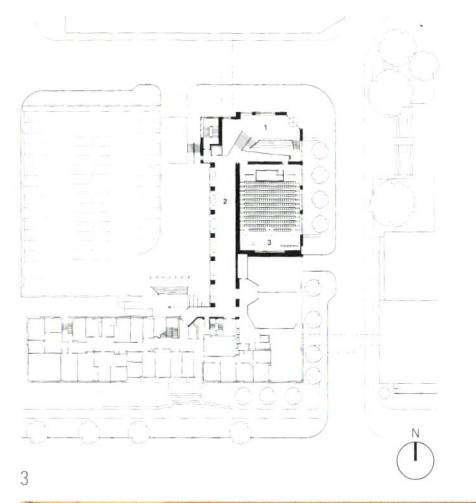

**Massachusetts Institute of Technology,
Tang Center for Management Education
Cambridge, Massachusetts, USA**
Ellenzweig Associates, Inc
1 Lecture hall
2 Case-study classroom
3 First floor plan
4 Lobby
5 View from northwest
6 Main entrance at dusk
Photo credit: Steve Rosenthal

**Massachusetts Institute of Technology,
Dorrance and Whitaker Buildings
Cambridge, Massachusetts, USA**
Ellenzweig Associates, Inc.

1 Computer centre
2 Flat-floor classroom
3 Multi-media lecture hall
4 Classroom entryway detail
5 Whitaker Building lobby with media wall

Photo credit: Steve Rosenthal

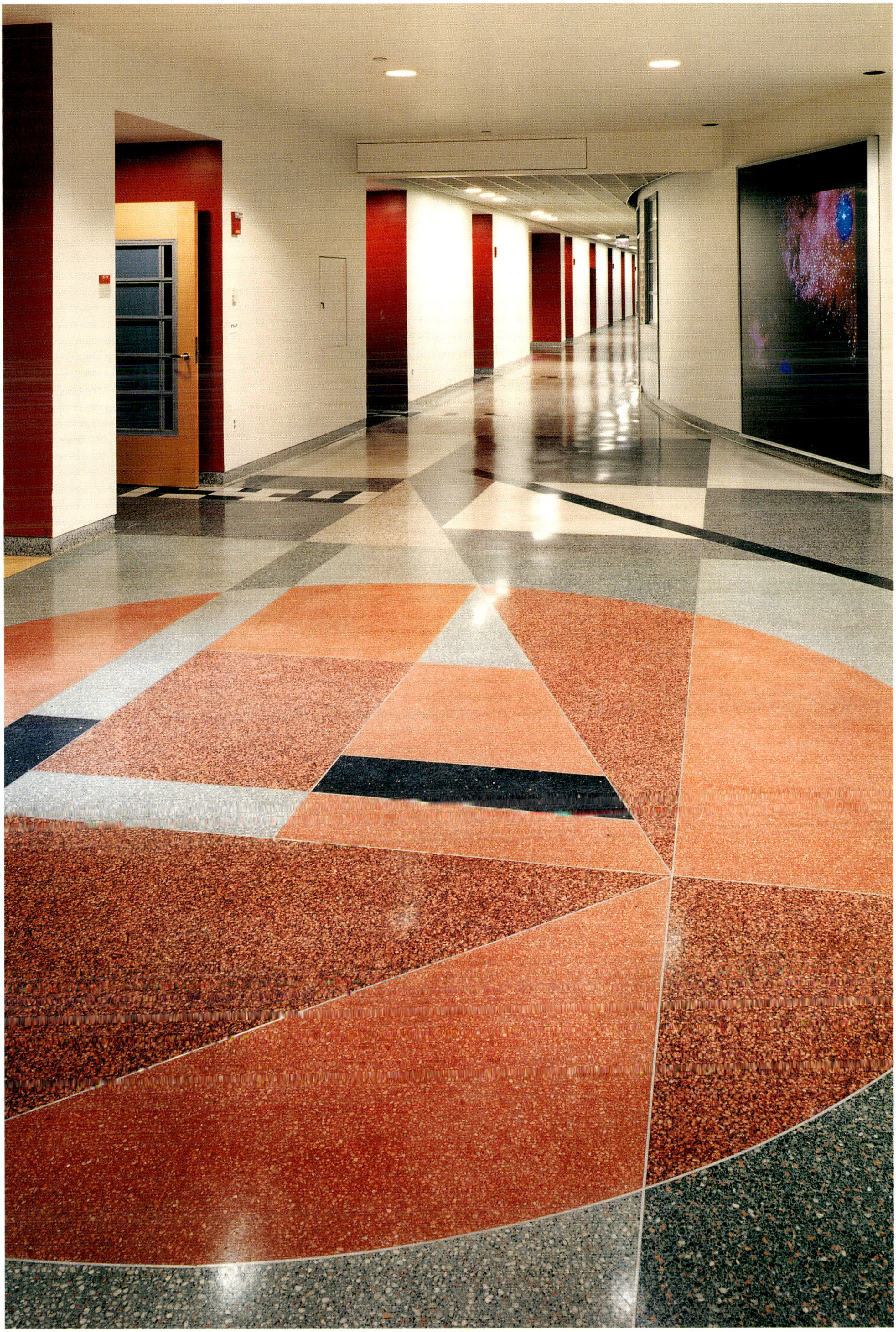

5

Capital Infocentre
Ottawa, Ontario, Canada
A.J. Diamond, Donald Schmitt and Company
1 Ceiling detail above interactive model
2 Double storey information media space
3 Itinerary planning stations suspended above original mosaic floor
4 Interactive model
Photo credit: Steven Evans

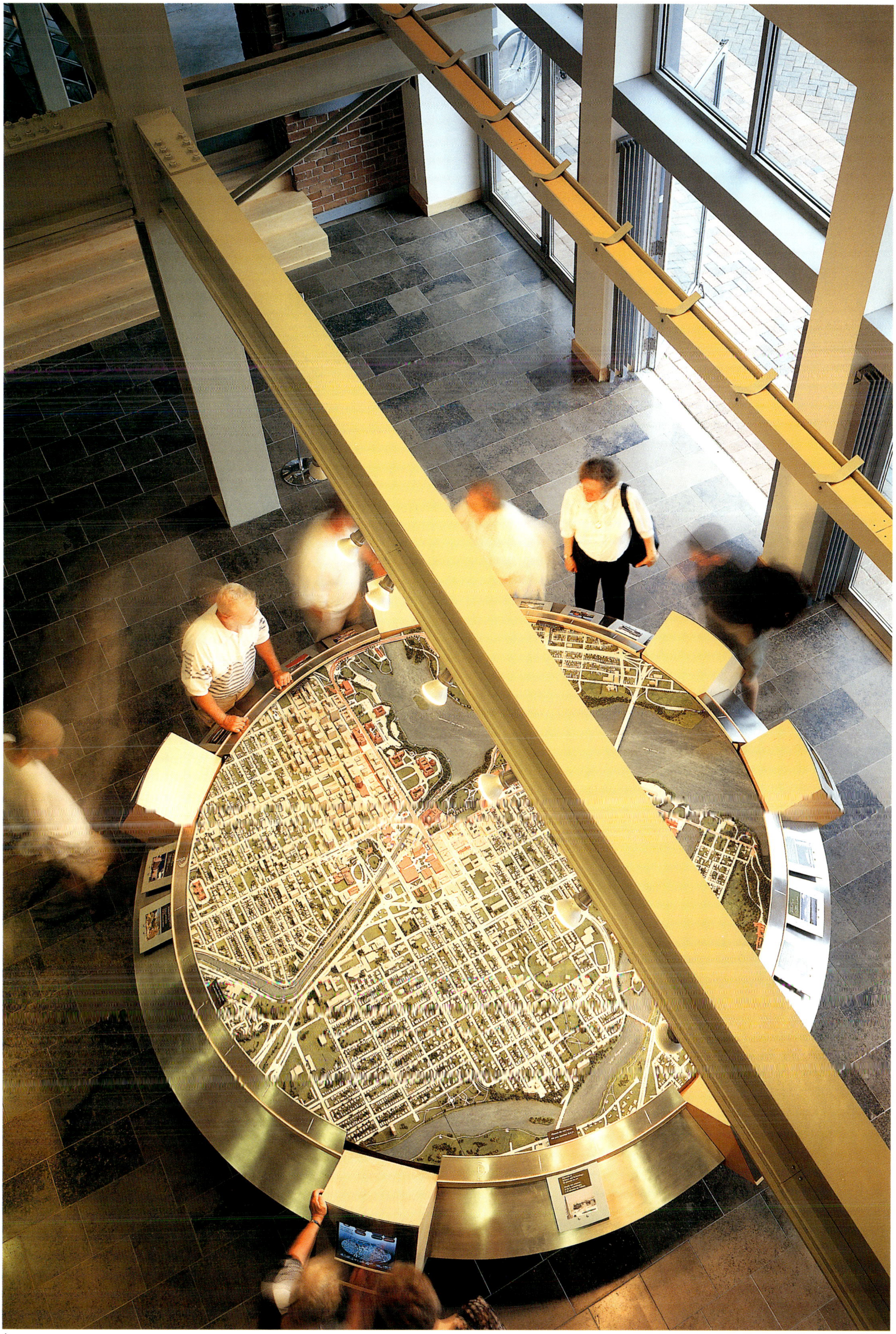

4

**The Kellogg Center, Albion College
Albion, Michigan, USA**
MacLachlan, Cornelius & Filoni, Inc.
Architects
1 Rear elevation, Dickie Hall now part of Center
2 Front elevation
3 Atrium looking toward living room
4 Multi-purpose room (formerly the Chapel)
5 Atrium, looking up to eyebrow window
Photo credit: Hedrich-Blessing

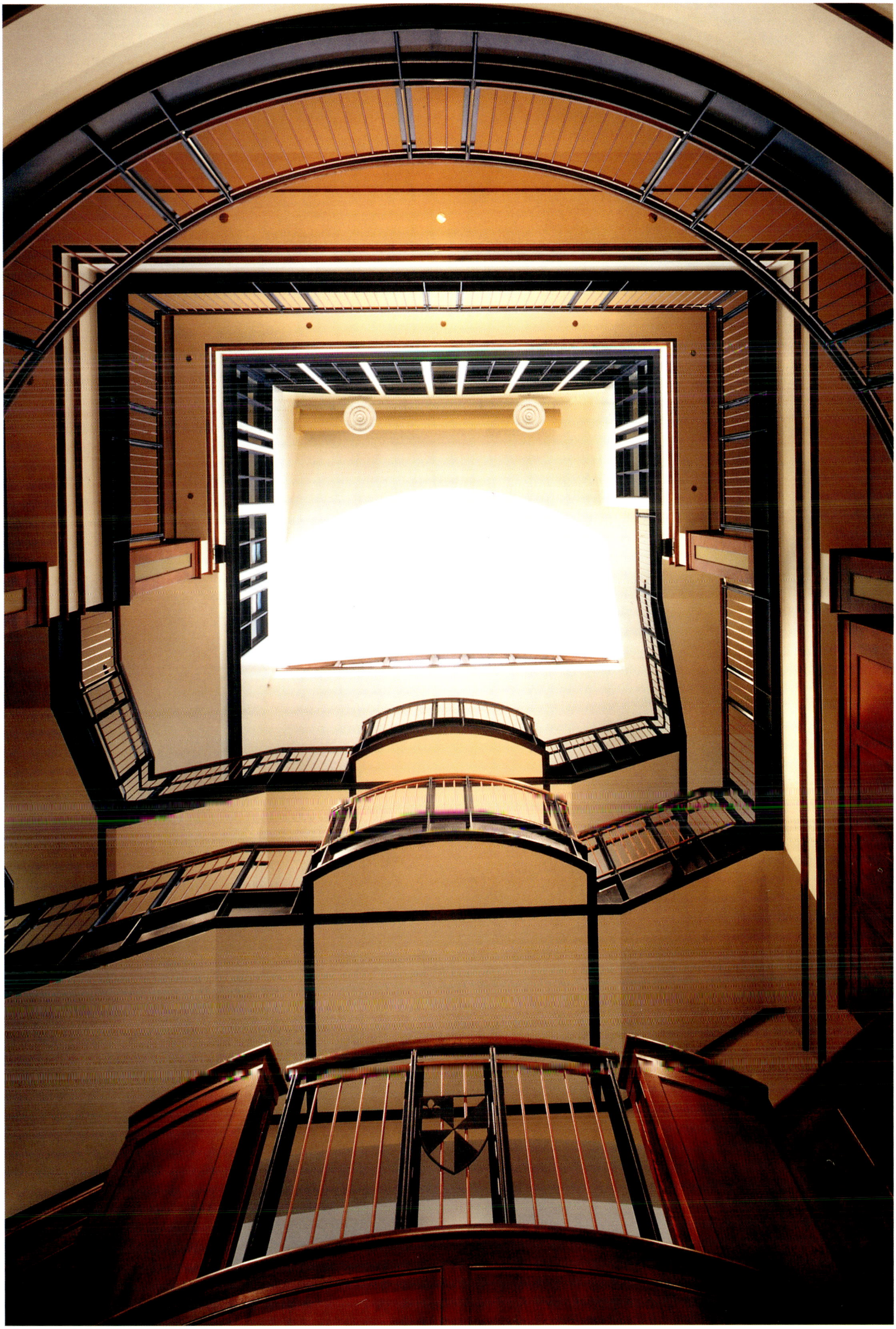

5

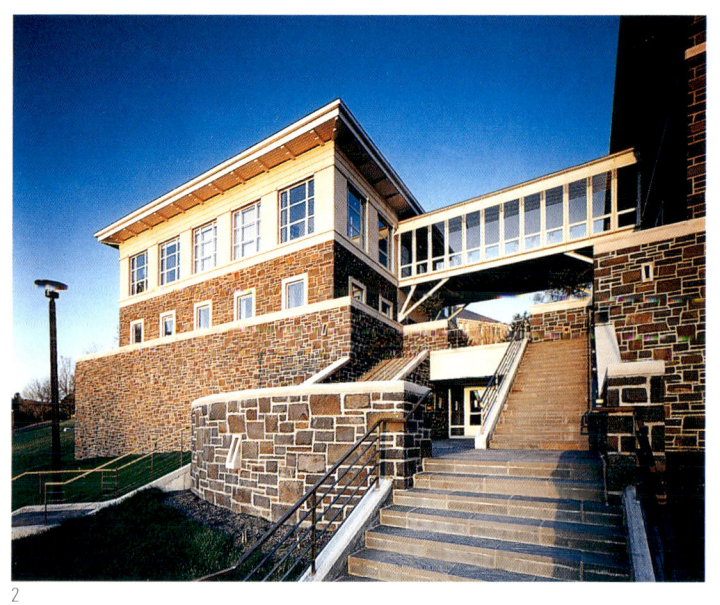

1

2

3

**Persson Hall, Colgate University
Hamilton, New York, USA**
Tai Soo Kim Partners, Architects
1　New building site bridges gap between upper and lower campus
2　Existing foot path dubbed "cardiac hill" divides building into two volumes
3　Building design features interior and exterior social spaces
4　Bridge connects classroom wing to faculty offices and lecture hall
5　Interiors are simply detailed and equipped for modern instruction
Photo credit: Nick Wheeler

Adult Education 157

Tsui Tsin Tong Building
Hong Kong
Nelson Chen Architects
1   Gallery level
2   Campus view with original museum in foreground
3   Gallery entrance hall
Opposite:
    Main atrium gallery with skylight above
Following Pages:
    Central monumental staircase connecting all gallery levels
Photo credit: Li Bun Photography

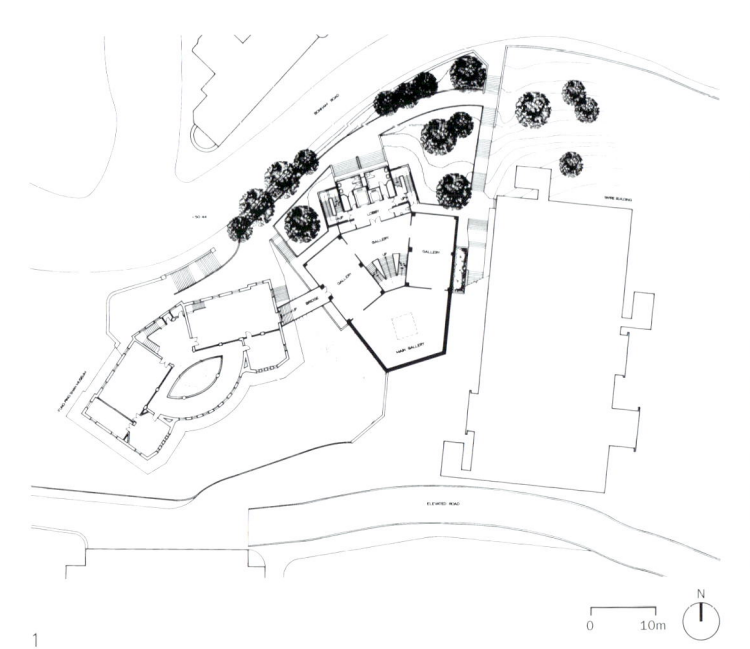

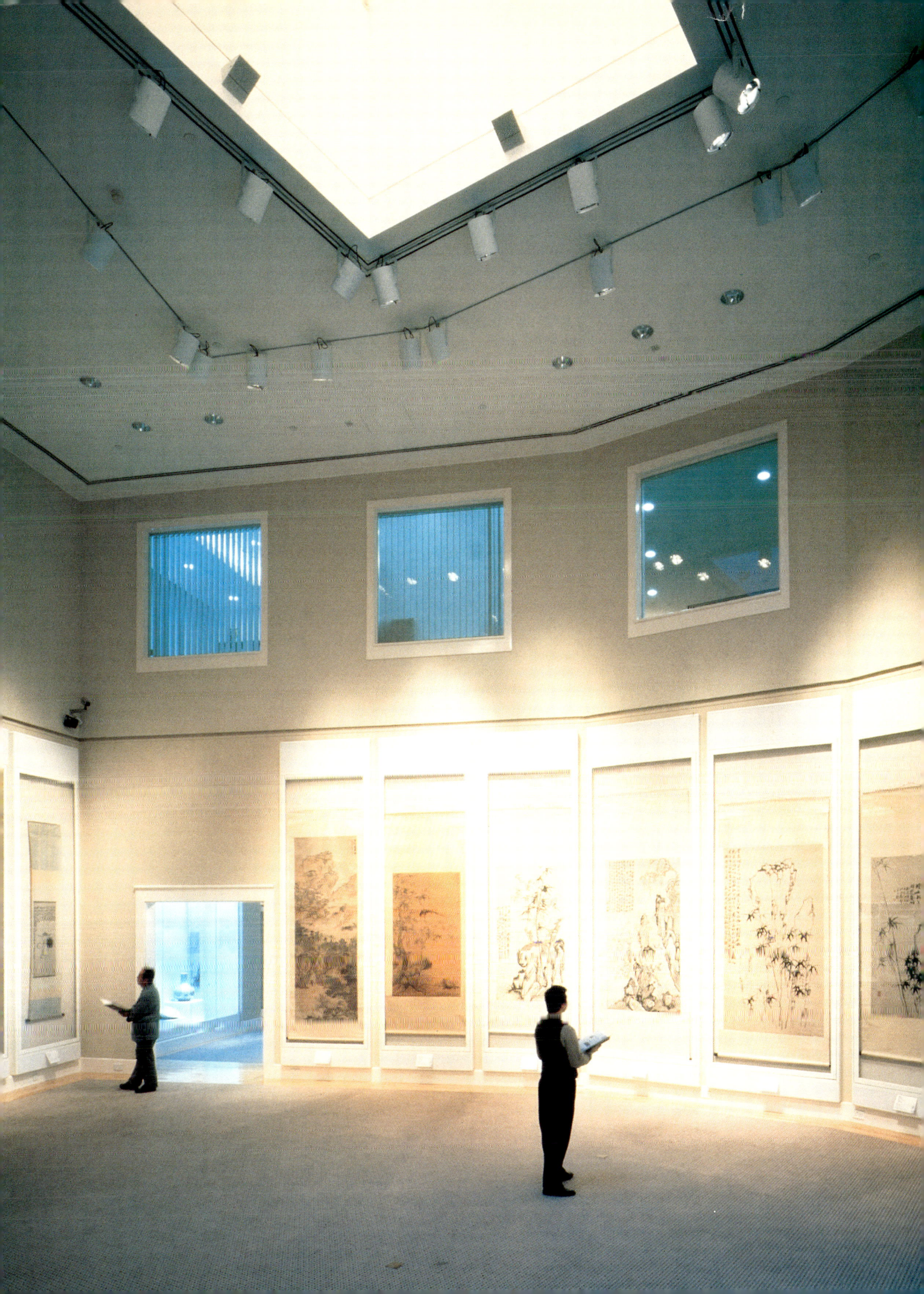

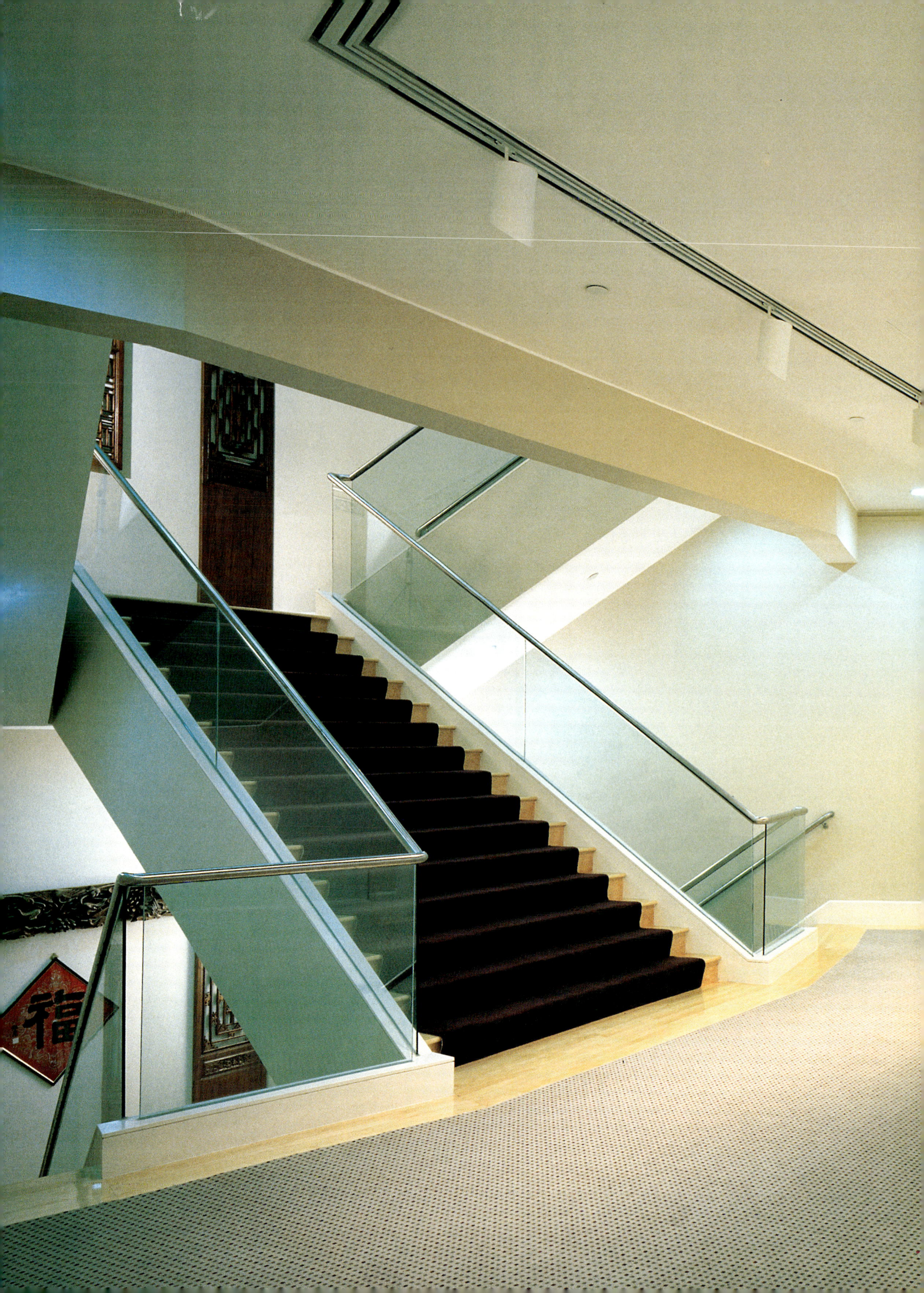
福

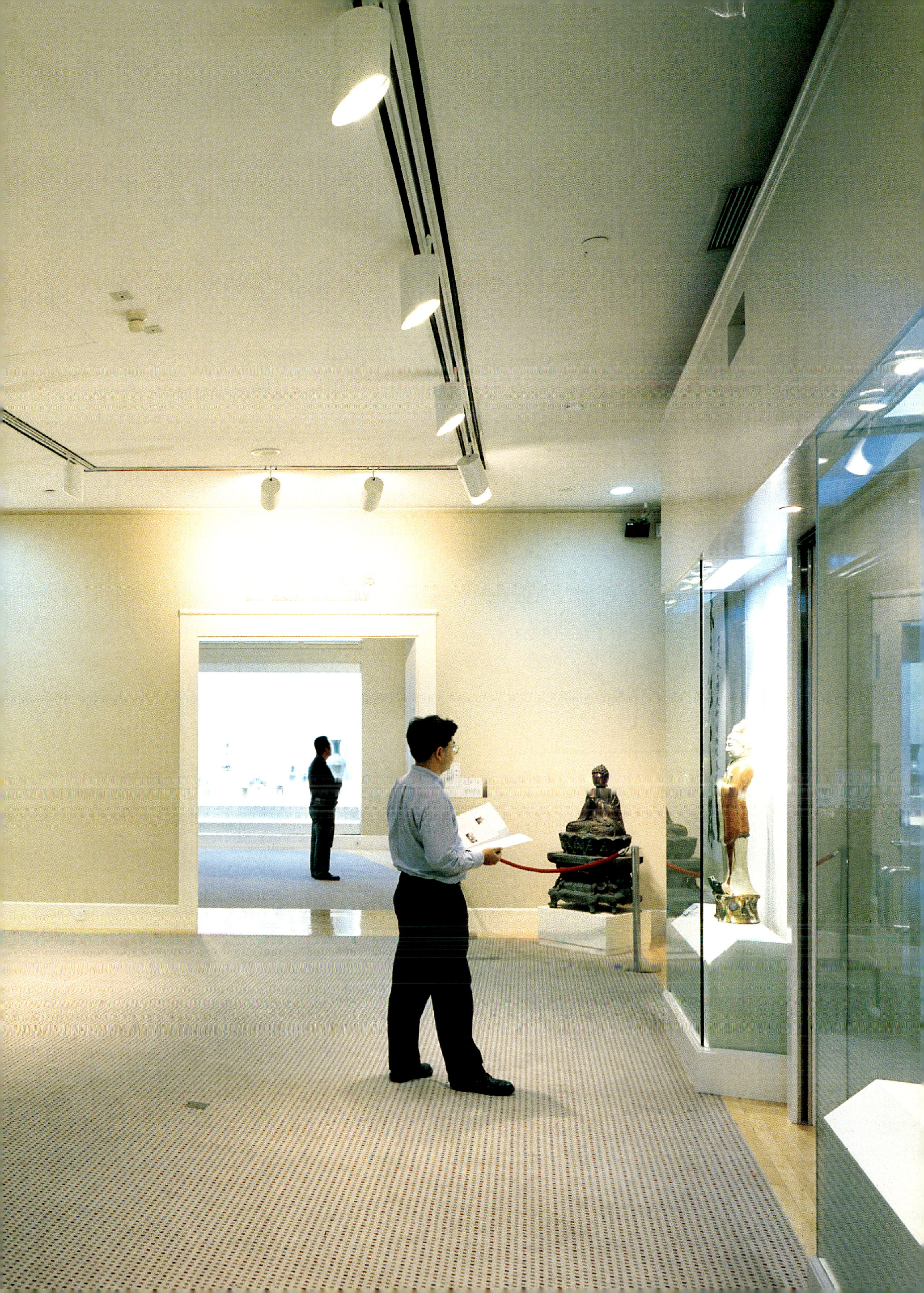

Kook Min Corporate Training Center
YoungIn, Korea
Tai Soo Kim Partners, Architects

1 Educational and residential program housed in separate buildings on site
2 Building elements mirror surrounding rolling hills
3 Seminar and instruction rooms are flexible and fully equipped
4 View of small courtyard to main entrance
5 Lobby interior featuring sculpture and skylight

Photo credit: Timothy Hursely

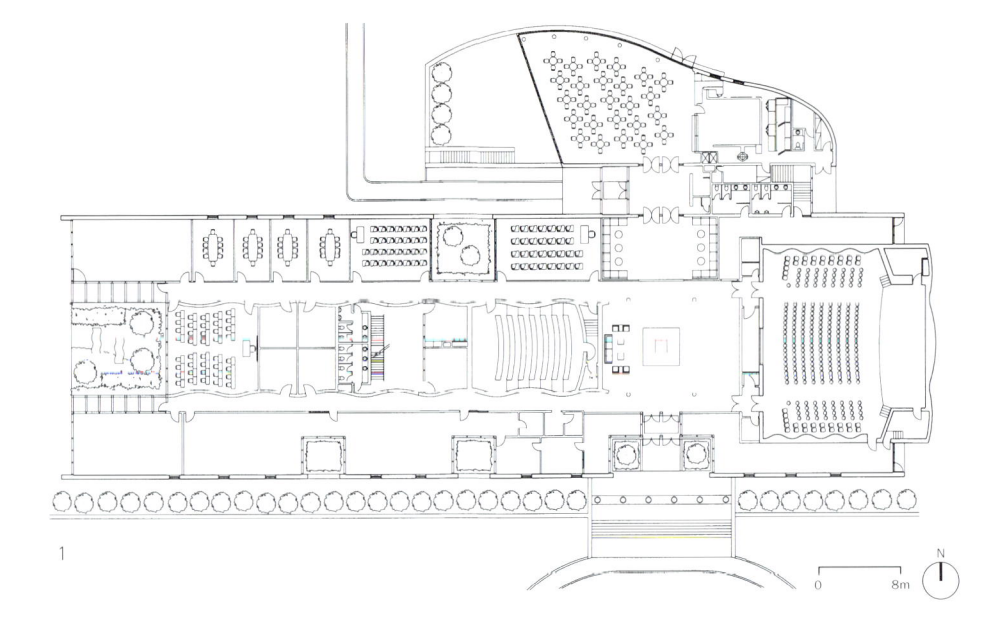

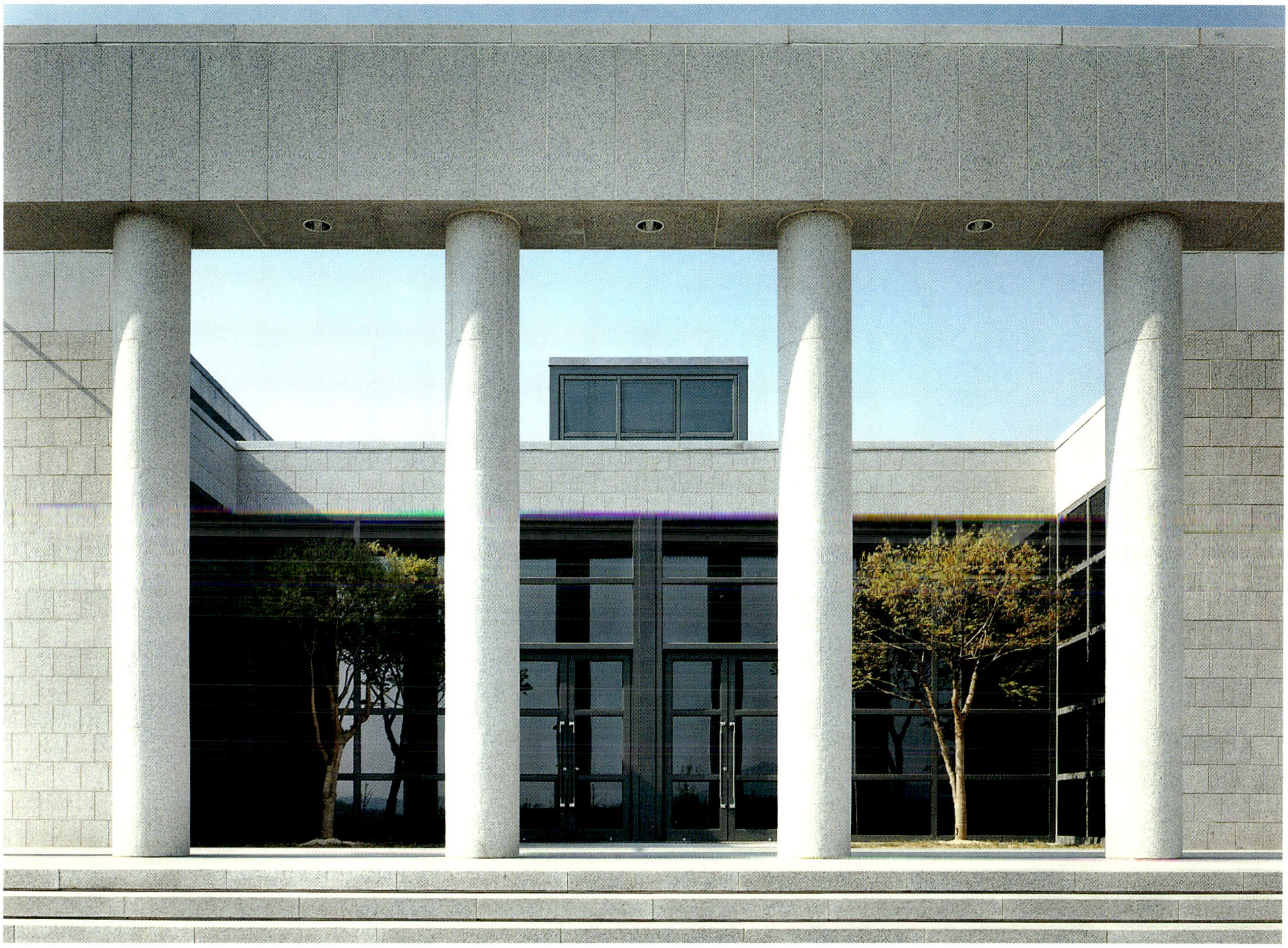

4

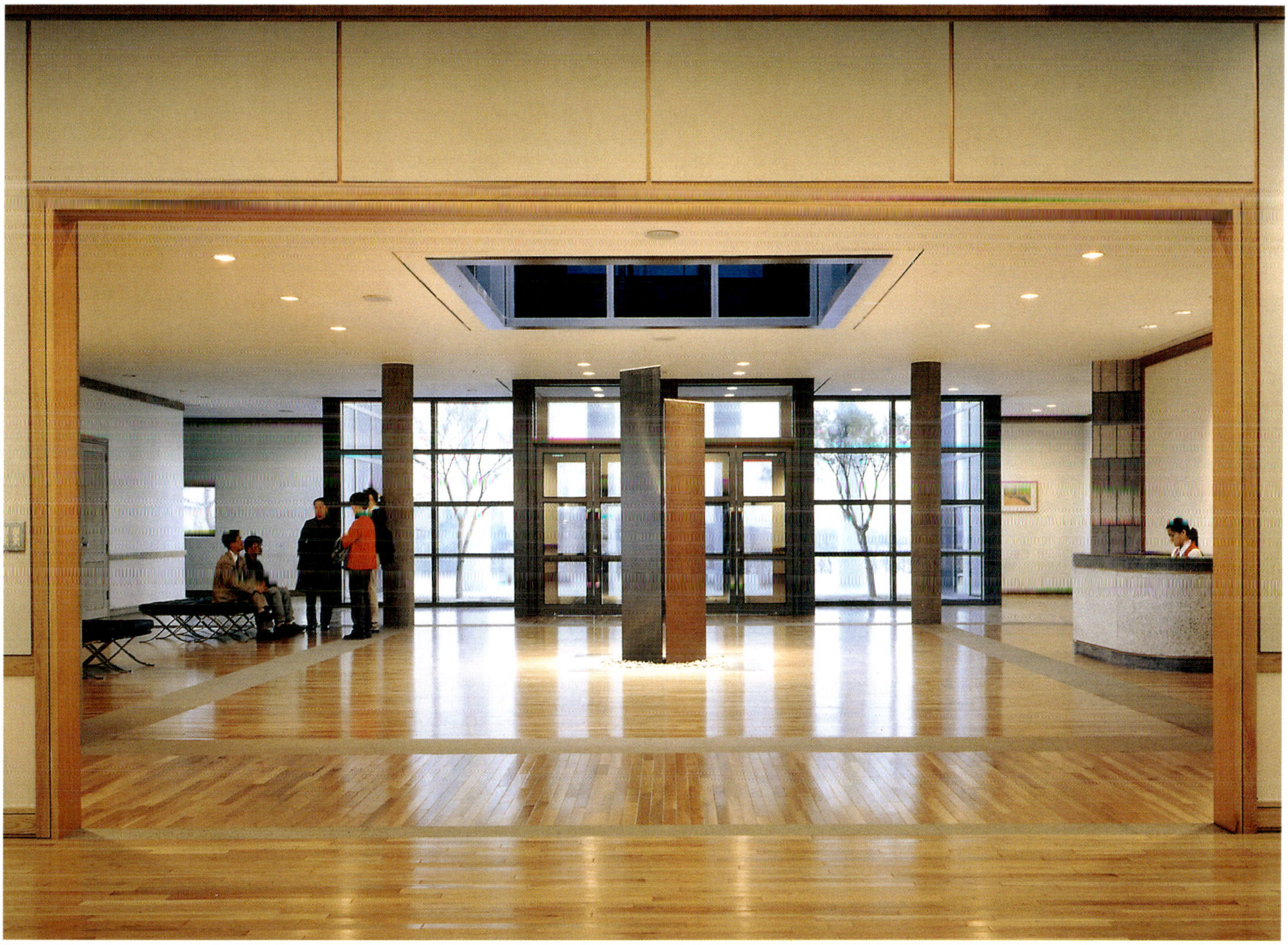

5

Northern Metropolitan College of TAFE
Greensborough, Melbourne, Australia
Williams & Boag Pty Ltd Architects
1   Main stair
2   Library entry
3   Entry lobby
Opposite:
    Library study area
Photo credit: John Gollings

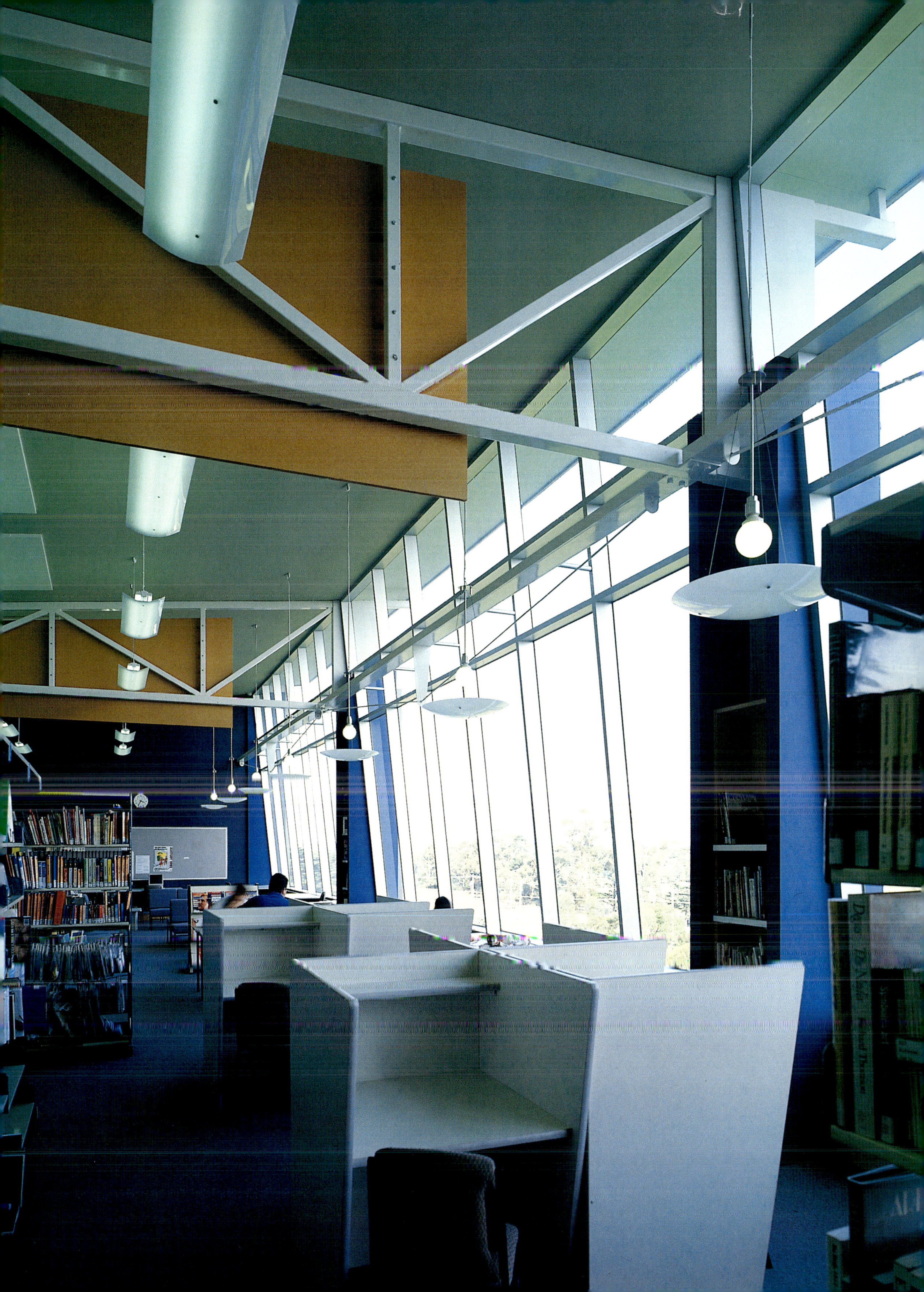

Open Training and Education Network, Technical and Further Education
NSW, Australia
Cox Richardson

1 Main entry and communication tower
2 Facade detail, office wing
3 Facade of entry
4 Internal courtyard
Photo credit: Patrick Bingham-Hall

Adult Education

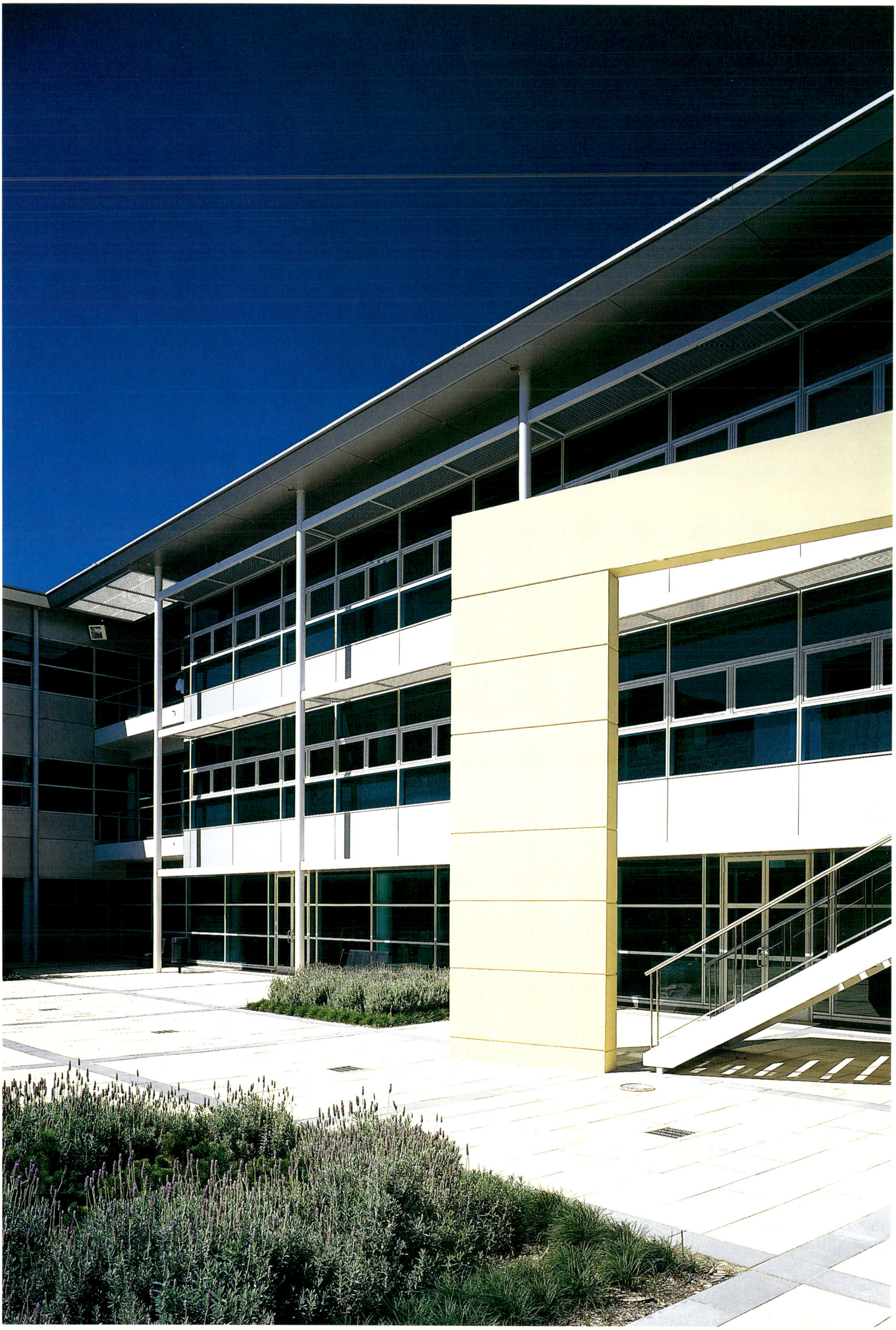

5

Open Training and Education Network, Technical and Further Education NSW, Australia
Cox Richardson

5 Office wing and landscaped court
6 Office pod from southern courtyard
Photo credit: Patrick Bingham-Hall

St Joseph's Institution Singapore
Alfred Wong Partnership Pte Ltd

7 Ceiling of the chapel
8 Overview of the sports field
9 Classroom blocks facade
10 Administration block corner detail
11 Chapel
Photo credit: courtesy Alfred Wong Partnership Pte Ltd

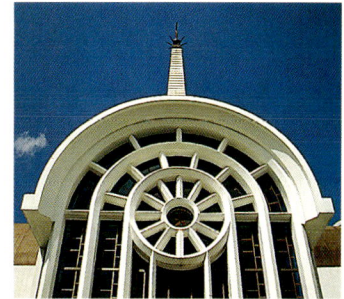

Adult Education 169

Howard E. LeFevre Hall,
Central Ohio Technical College/Ohio State University
Ohio, USA
NBBJ

1 Entrance
2 Central corridor
3 View from south
4 Exterior wall detail
Photo credit: Timothy Hursley

4

1
2
3
4

**Glasgow Caledonian University,
Extension to the William Harley Library
Glasgow, Scotland, UK**
Austin-Smith:Lord

1 Entrance hall with security line
2 Main counter and reference area
3 Entry atrium from north
4 Route from ground floor reading room

Photo credit: Renzo Mazzolini

**Cornwall Public Library
Cornwall, Ontario, Canada**
A.J. Diamond, Donald Schmitt and Company

5 Building exterior
6 Periodicals room with marble panelling

Photo credit: Steven Evans

Adult Education 173

Cornwall Public Library
Cornwall, Ontario, Canada
A.J. Diamond, Donald Schmitt and Company
7   Display cabinets in public corridor
8   Reading tables in stacks
Photo credit: Steven Evans

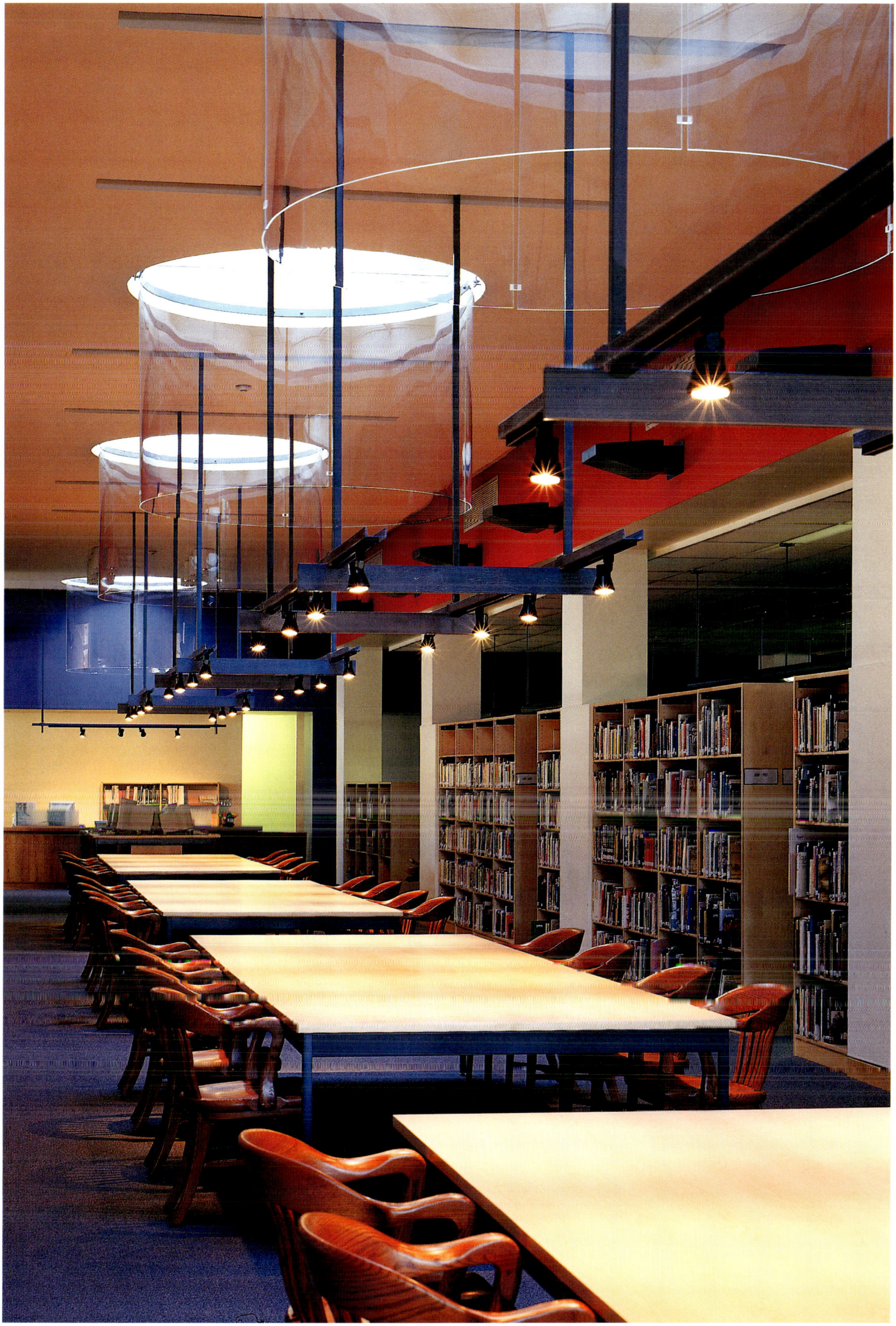

8

Catholic University Library and Lecture Hall
Seoul, Korea
Kunchook - Moonhwa Architects & Engineers
1   Ground floor plan
2   Entrance of library
3   View on approach road
4   Exterior scene of library
Photo credit: courtesy Kunchook - Moonhwa Architects & Engineers

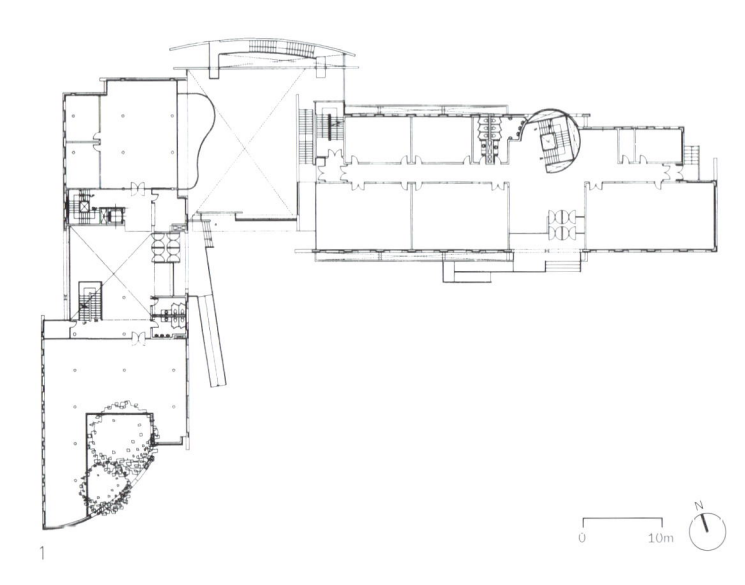

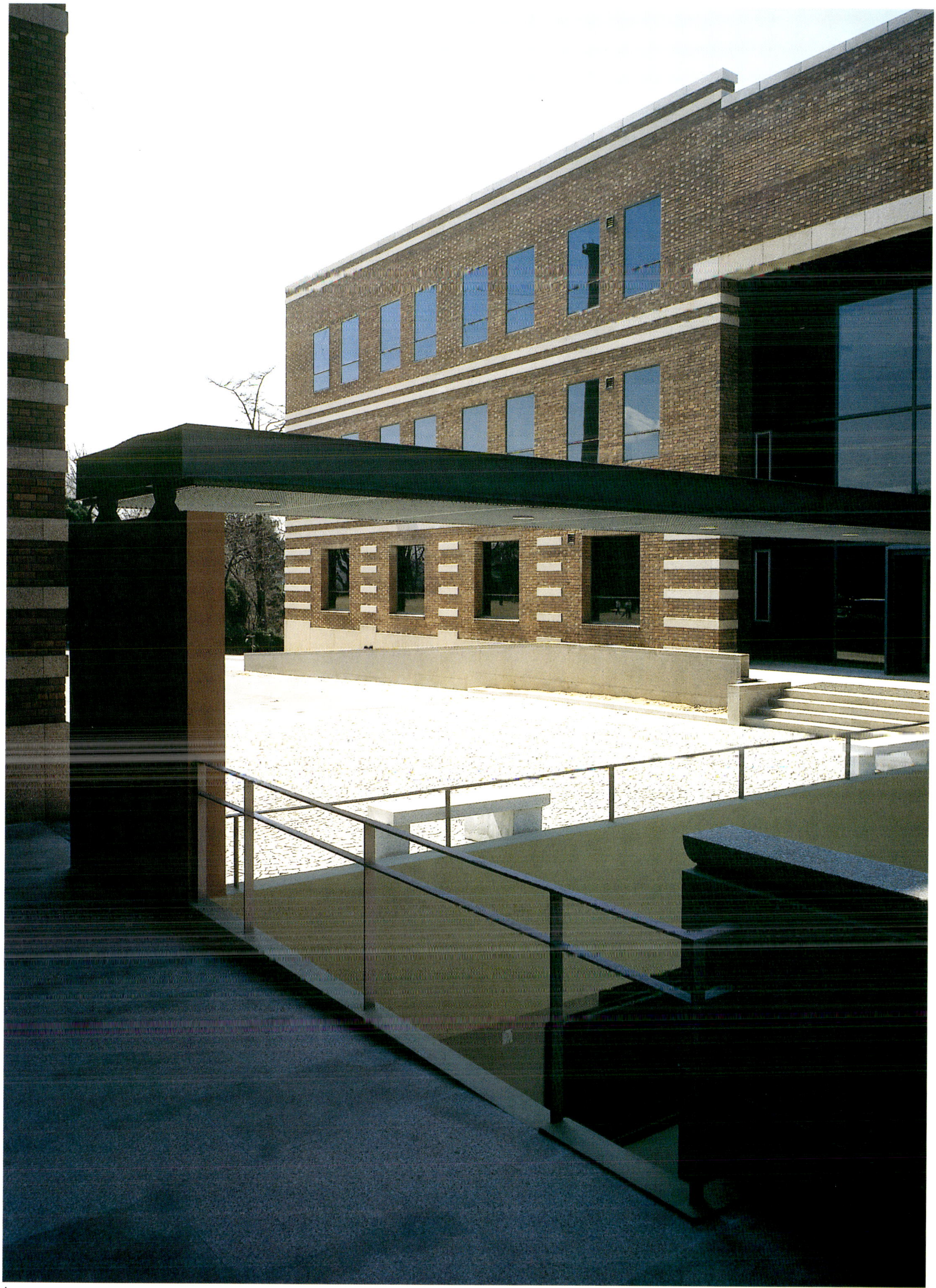

4

**Catholic University Library and Lecture Hall
Seoul, Korea**
Kunchook - Moonhwa Architects & Engineers
5   Large window in entrance hall
6   Interior scene entrance hall of library
7   Connection room between library K and lecture hall
Photo credit: courtesy Kunchook - Moonhwa Architects & Engineers

7

Richmond Hill Central Library
Richmond Hill, Ontario, Canada
A.J. Diamond, Donald Schmitt and Company

1 Richmond Hill front facade
2 Double-storey reference room
3 Public stair system
4 South facade reading room

Photo credit: Steven Evans

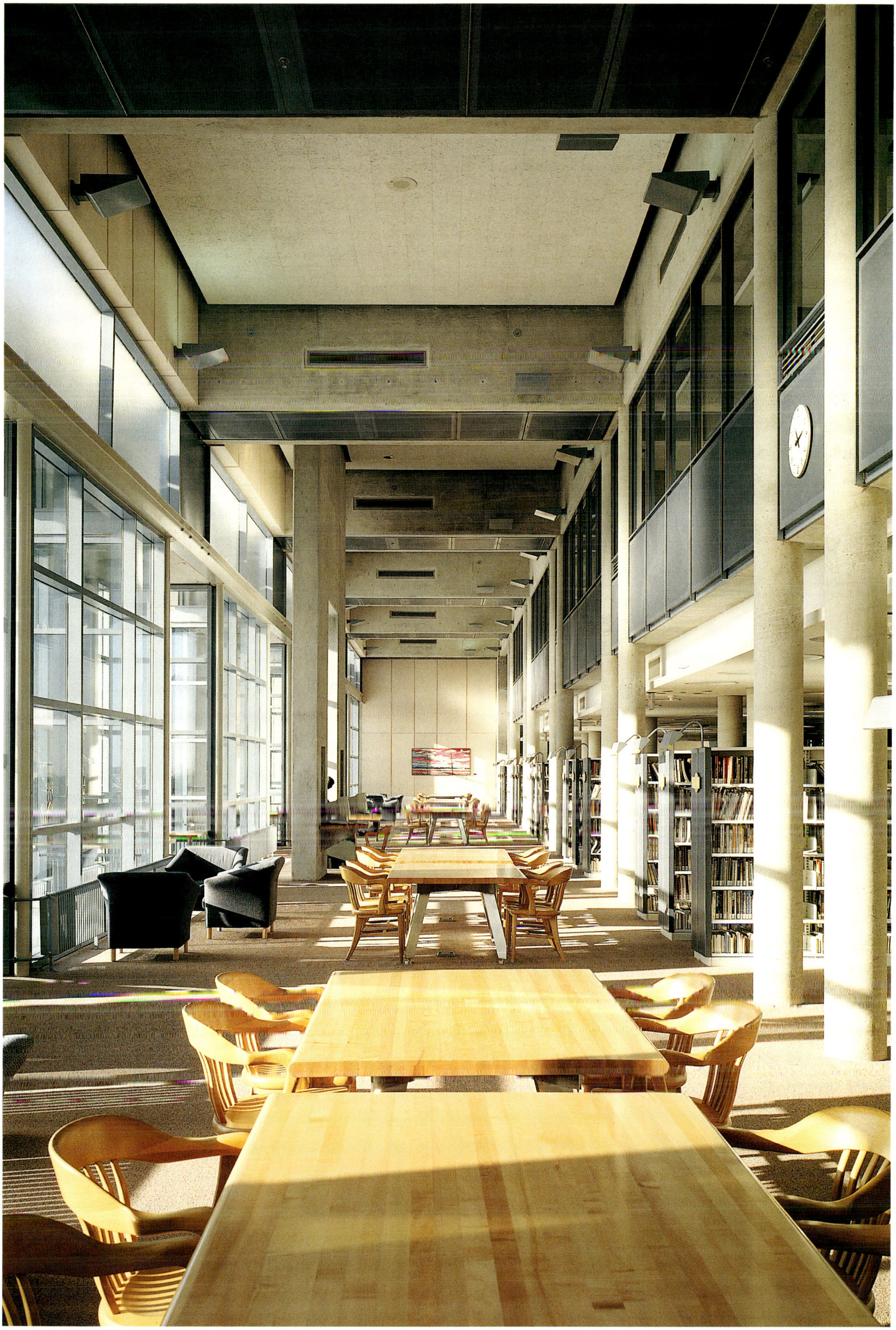

4

Cranfield University Library
Befordshire, UK
Foster and Partners
1 Entrance Canopy
2 Ground floor plan
3 First floor library
4 Magazine library
5 Exterior at night
6 Perimeter study carrels
Photo credit: courtesy Foster and Partners

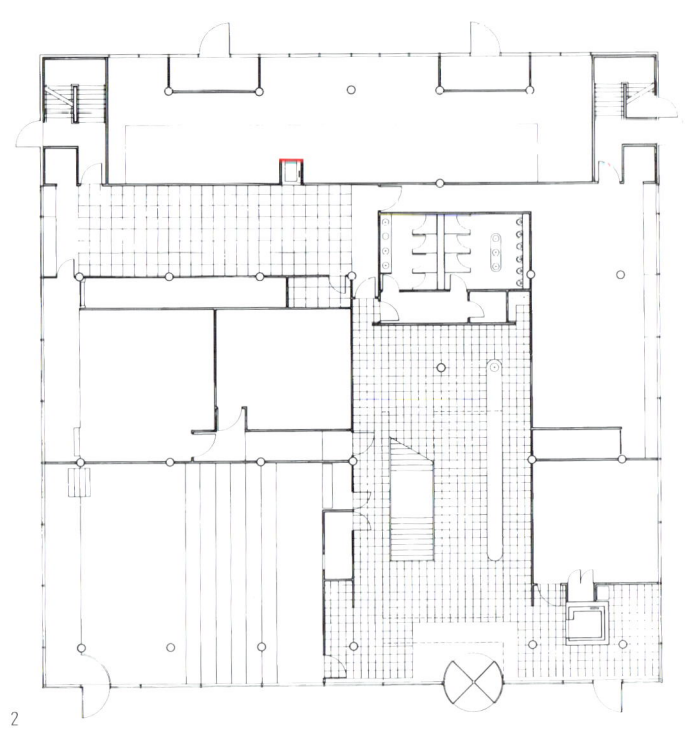

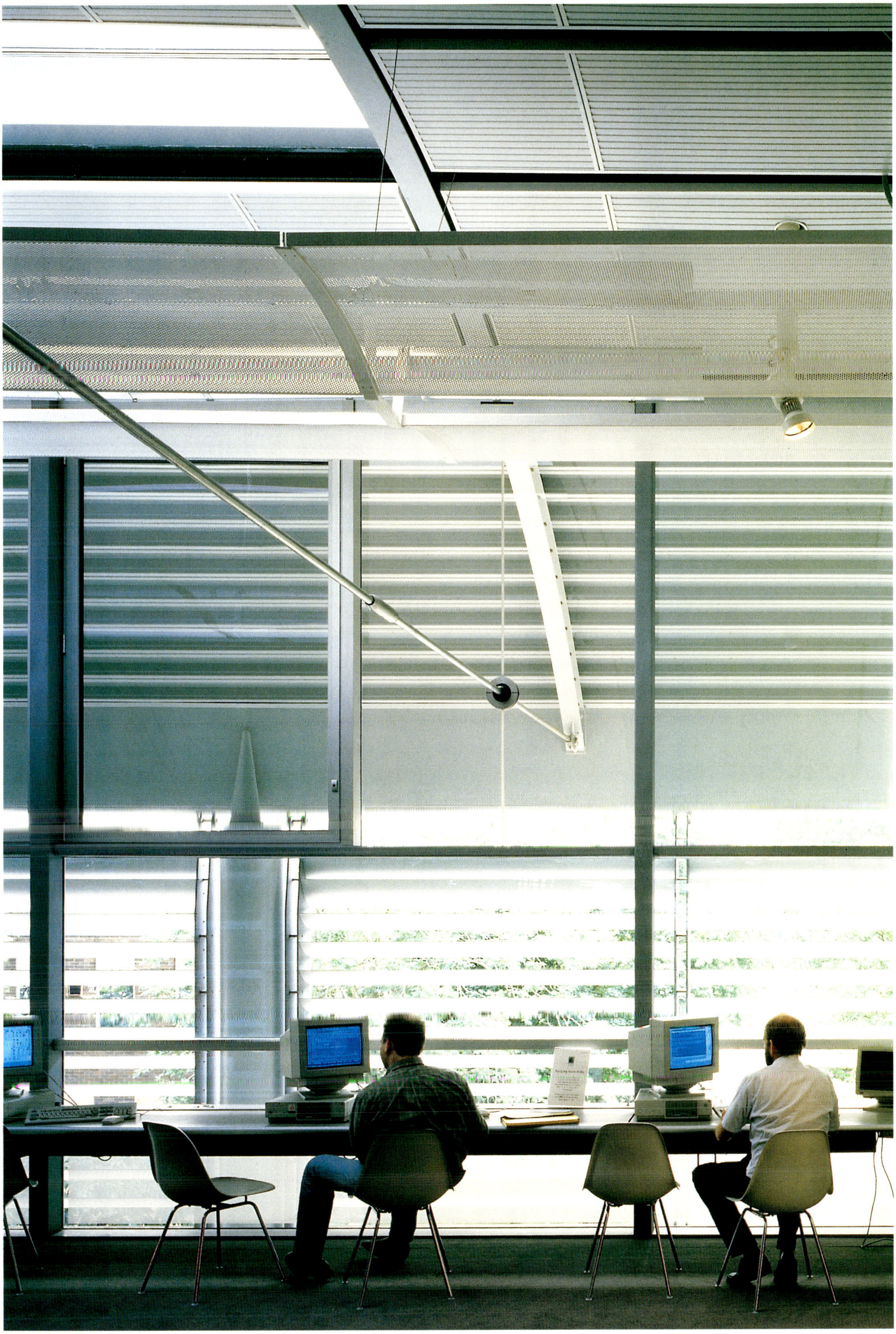

6

Center Hall, University of California, San Diego Classroom Building I
San Diego, California, USA
NBBJ

1. Typical classroom lecture hall
2. Primary entrance, northwest corner
3. View of west wing looking southeast
4. View of north wing looking southwest
5. Detail of colonnade, west wing

Photo credit: Timothy Hursley

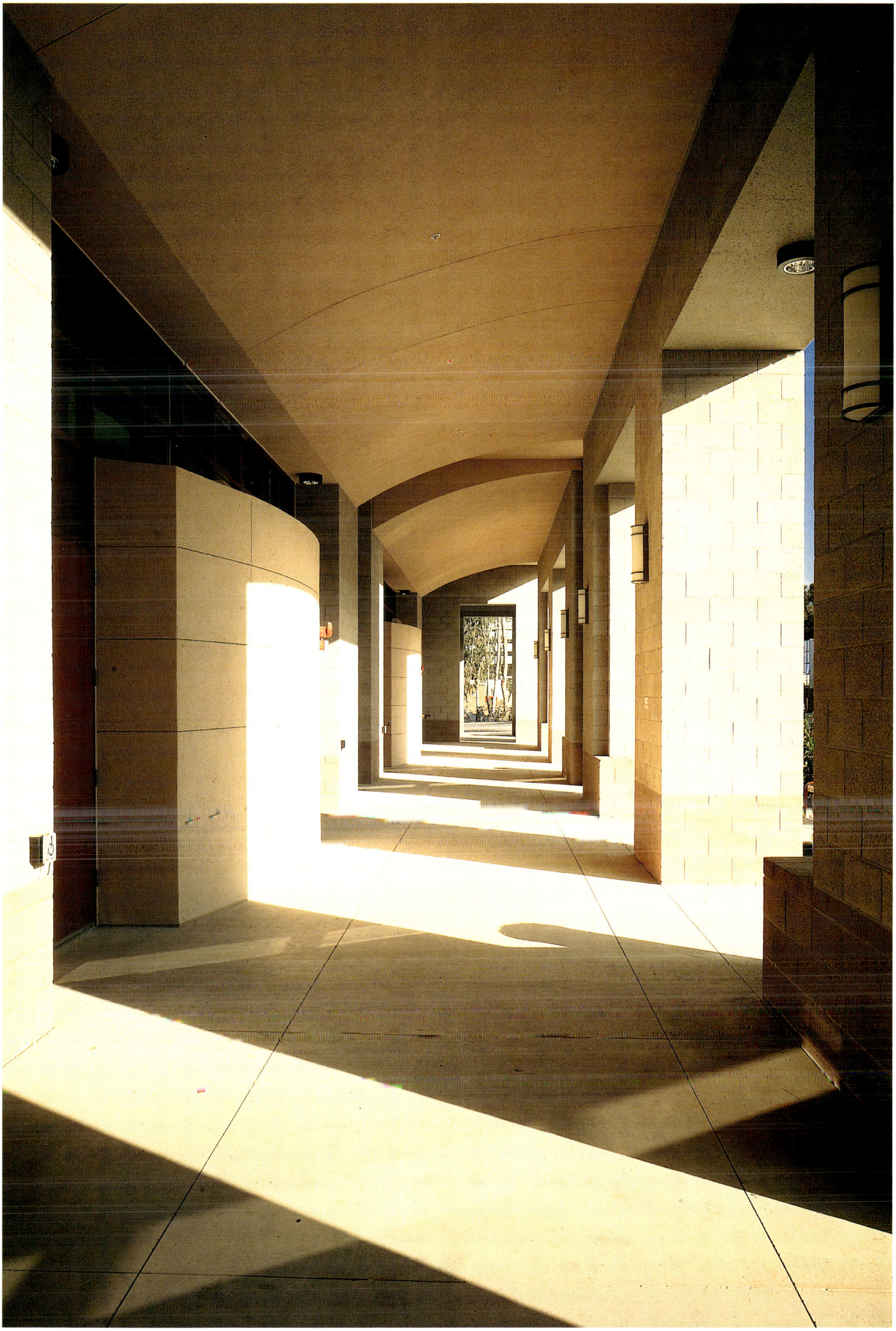

5

The Education Building
Sydney, NSW, Australia
Ancher Mortlock and Woolley
1   Glazing system supported from external steel truss
2   Junction of curved, glazed atrium and glazed walkway
3   Level 2 atrium lobby
Photo credit: Tim Collis-Bird (1,2); Eric Sierins (3)

Rijksakademie van Beeldende Kunsten
Netherlands
Architektenburo K. van Velsen B.V.
4 – 6   Various views of courtyard
Photo credit: Michel Boesveld

4

5

6

**Extension to First Buildings,
Warwick University
Conventry, UK**
Shepheard Epstein Hunter

1 New toplit atrium behind existing lecture theatre
2 New lecture theatre
3 New toplit atrium behind existing lecture theatre

Photo credit: courtesy Shepheard Epstein Hunter

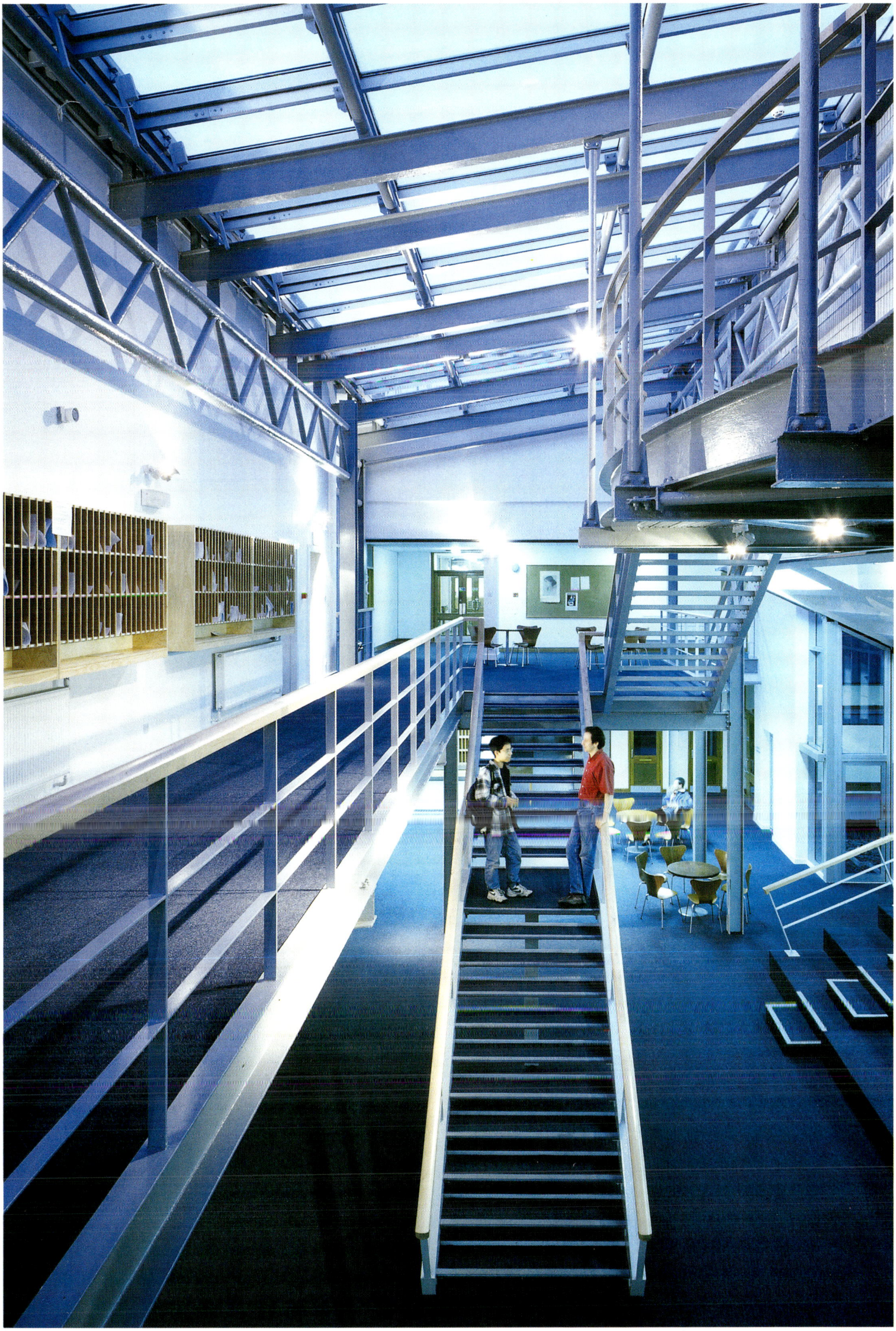

3

**Center for Molecular Electronics,
University of Missouri
St. Louis, Missouri, USA**
Mackey Mitchell Associates

1   Northwest elevation
2   Research laboratory
3   First floor conference room
4   North elevation
5   View to lake from second floor lounge
6   First floor stairwell and seating area

Photo credit: Sam Fentress

5

6

Woodsworth College, University of Toronto
Toronto, Ontario, Canada
Barton Myers Associates, Inc./KPMB
Joint Venture Architects

1   Corridor between cafe and college offices
2   Interior corridor opening directly to the courtyard
3   View looking southeast toward new building's main entrance
4   The skylit and dynamically curving cafe/bar
Photo credit: Steven Evans

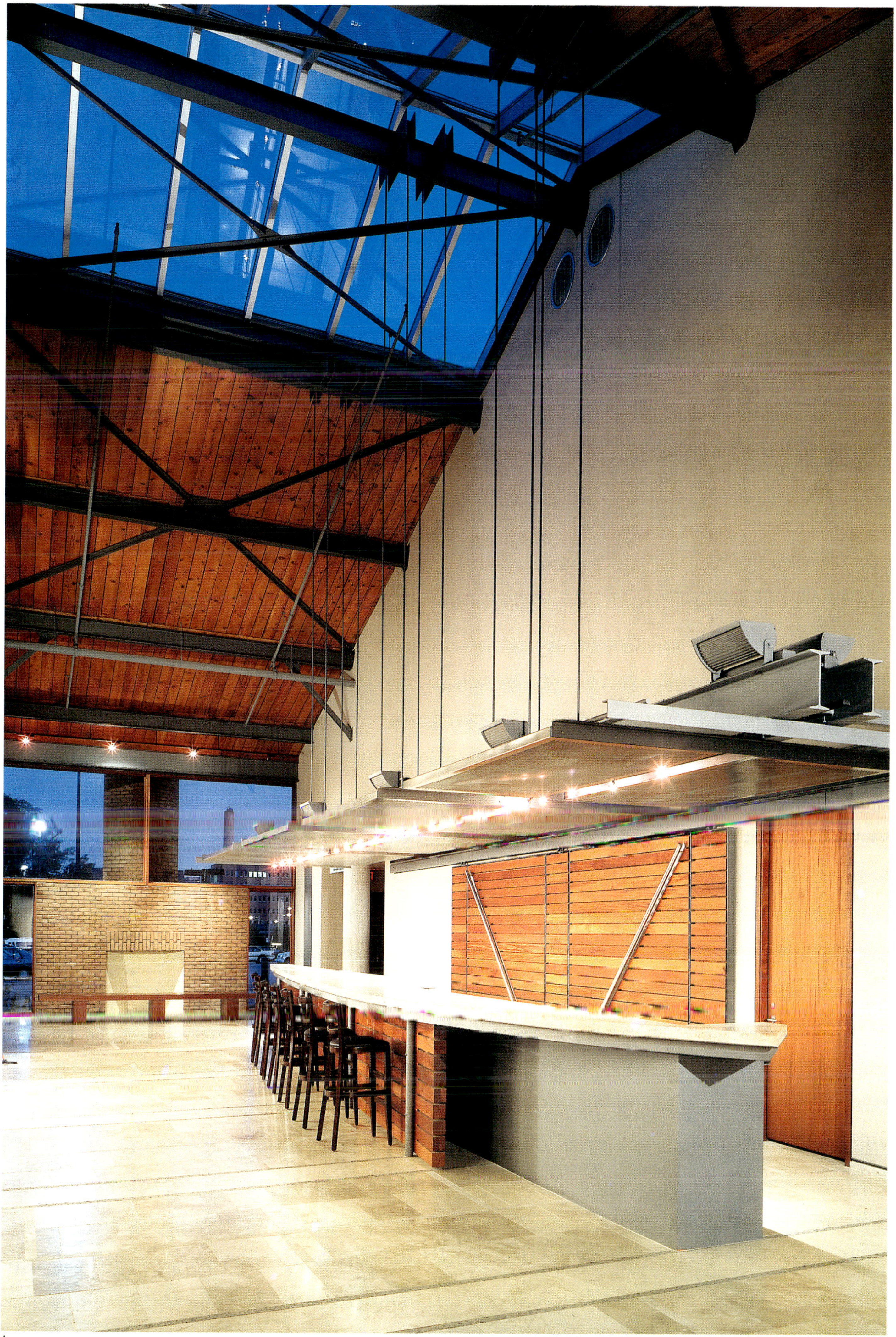

4

Noble Hall, Eastern Connecticut State University
Willimantic, Connecticut, USA
Du Bose Associates Inc., Architects
1   New reception/lobby area
Photo credit: Robert Benson Photography

New Classroom Building
Eastern Connecticut State University
Willimantic, Connecticut, USA
Du Bose Associates Inc., Architects
2   Front elevation
Photo credit: Robert Benson Photography

Swing Space Building
Southern Conneticut State University
New Haven, Connecticut, USA
Du Bose Associates Inc., Architects
3   Front elevation
4   Entrance foyer
Photo credit: Robert Benson Photography

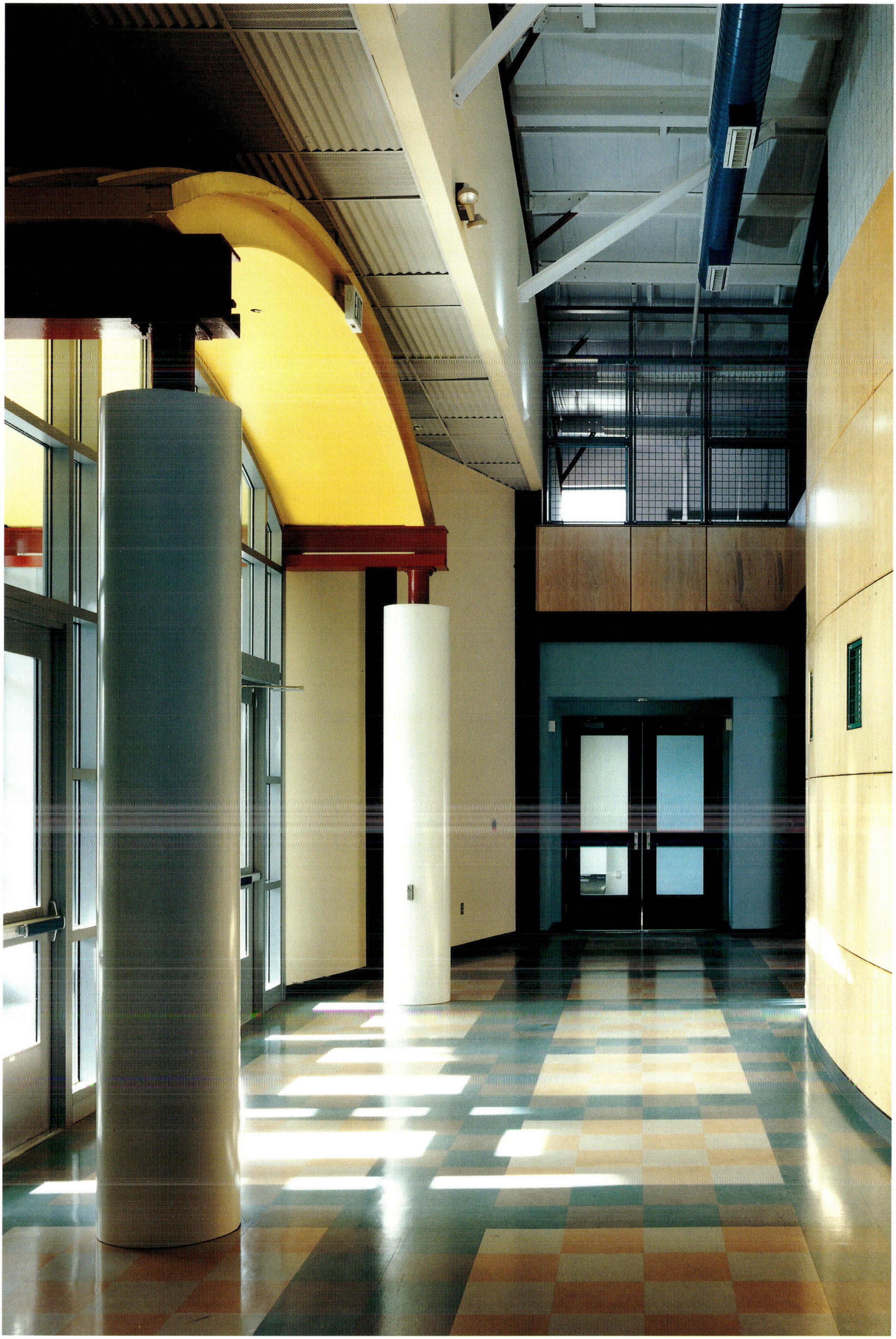

4

Cyberia Internet Cafe
Bangkok, Thailand
Blauel Architects, London

1 Ground floor plan
2 External night-time view
3 View along double height screen
4 View across cafe
5 Double height space
6 Overlooking cafe from bridge
7 Stairs to first floor
8 View through cafe towards entrance

Photo credit: Somkid Paimpiyachat, art4d—Bangkok

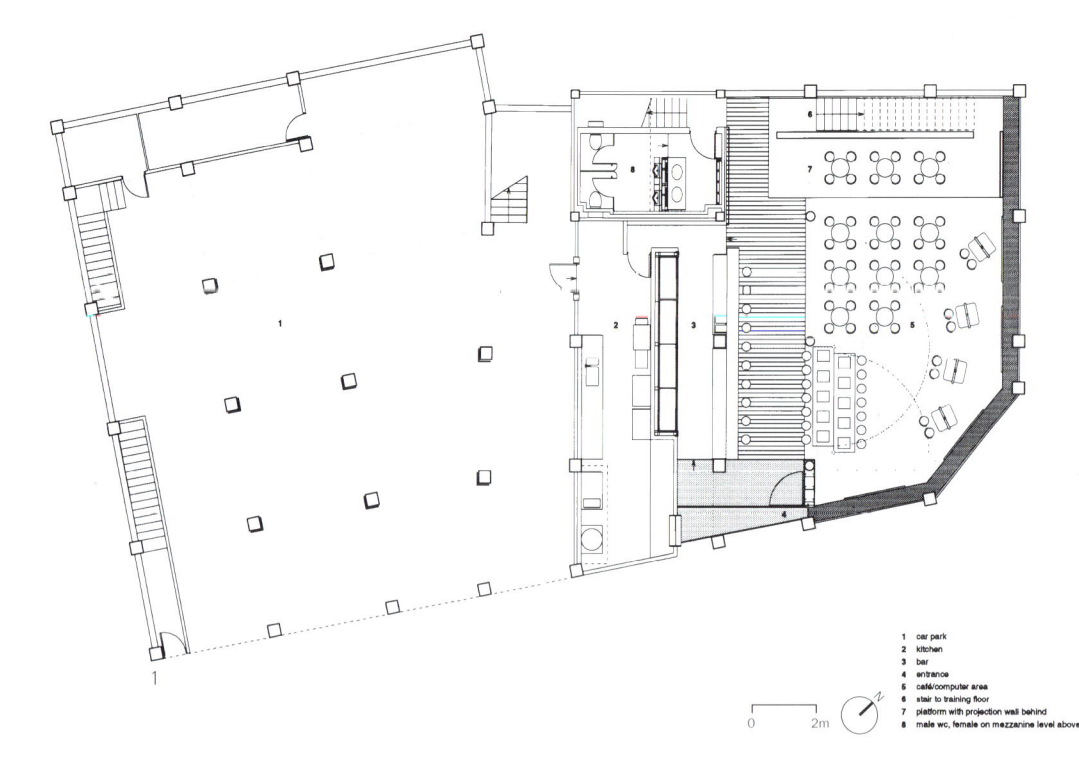

1 car park
2 kitchen
3 bar
4 entrance
5 café/computer area
6 stair to training floor
7 platform with projection wall behind
8 male wc, female on mezzanine level above

6

7

8

Pitzer College
Edith and Eli Broad Center
Claremont, California, USA
Gwathmey Siegel & Associates Architects
1   West facade public entry
2   Exhibition gallery
3   Stairwell
4   Second level reception
5   President's office
Photo credit: Assassi Productions

3

4

5

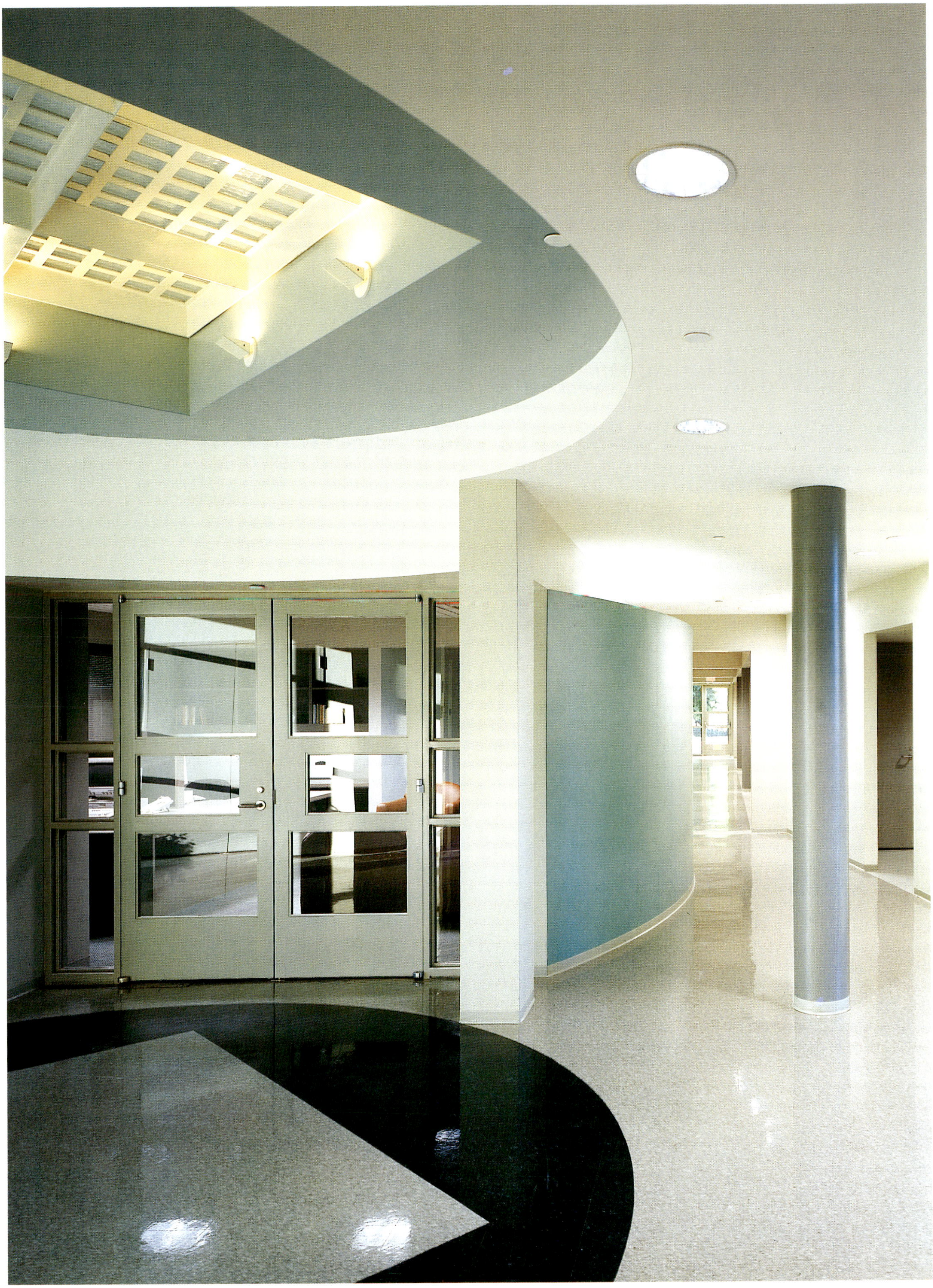

Pitzer College
Edith and Eli Broad Center
Claremont, California, USA
Gwathmey Siegel & Associates Architects
6 Ground floor lobby
7 Typical classroom
8 Performance/lecture space
Photo credit: Assassi Productions

Pitzer College
Gold Student Activity Center
Claremont, California, USA
Gwathmey Siegel & Associates Architects
Following Page:
   Snack bar
Photo credit: Assassi Productions

7

8

Adult Education 209

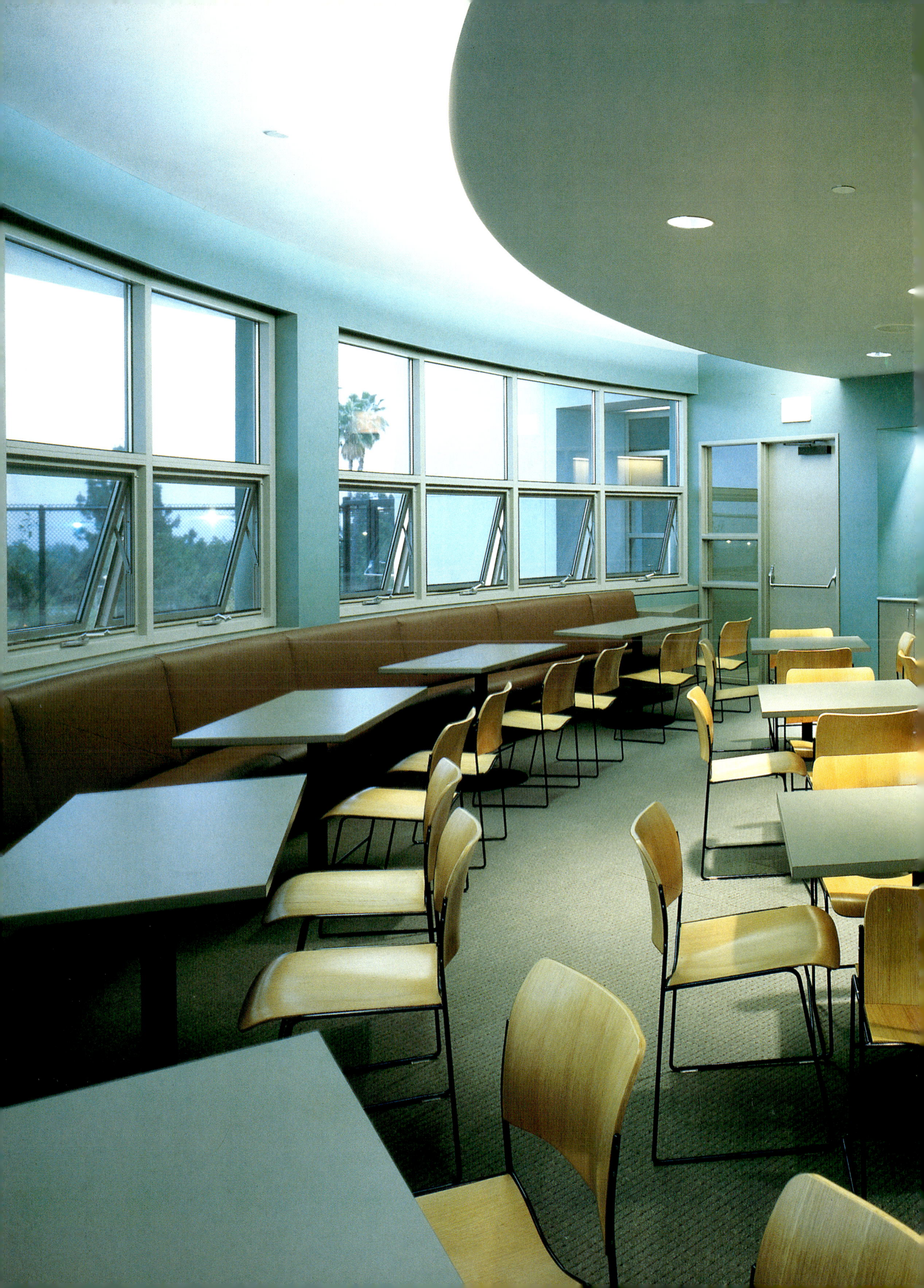

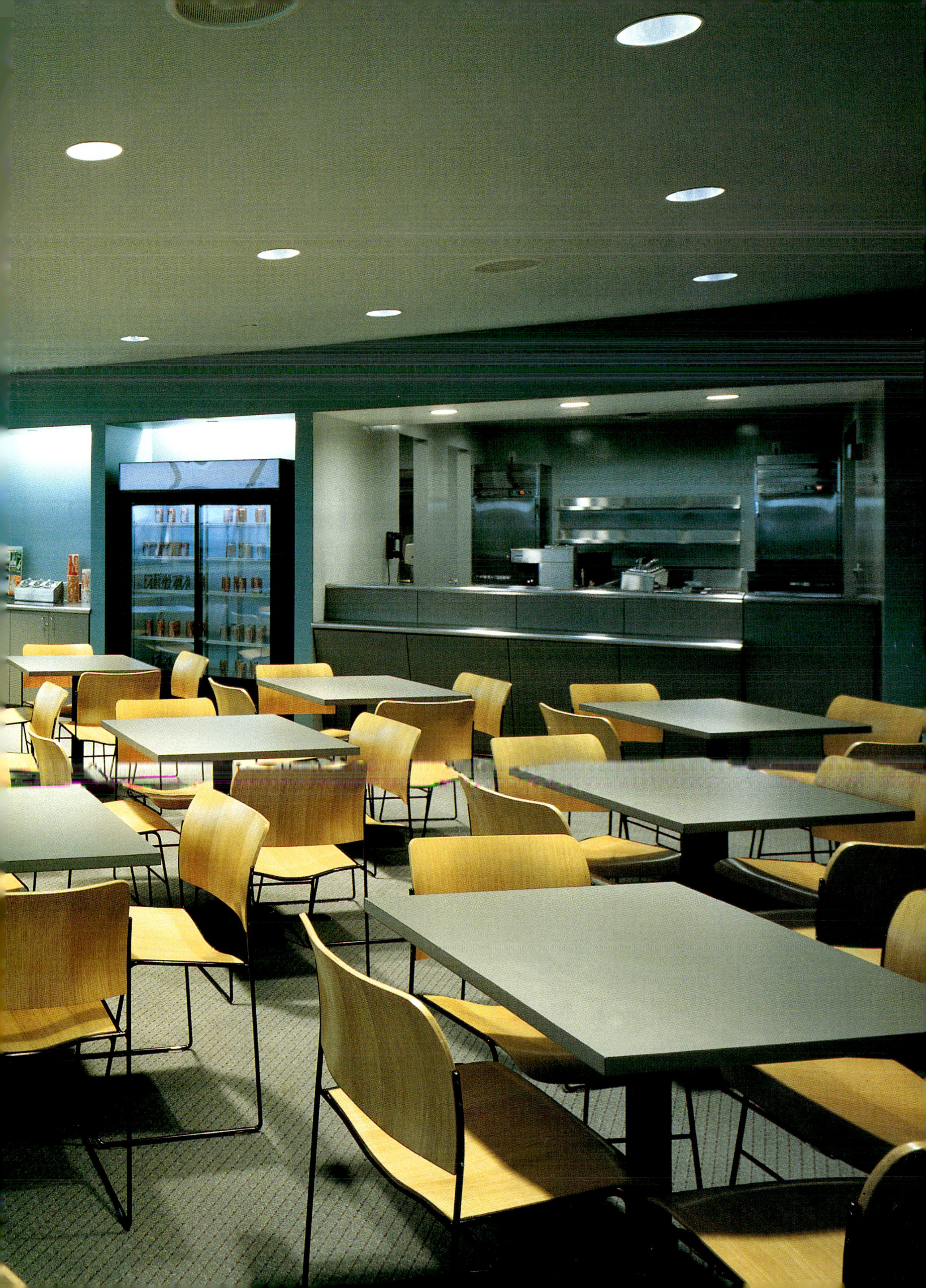

*"The loftiest edifices need the
deepest foundations"*
– George Santayana

Biographies

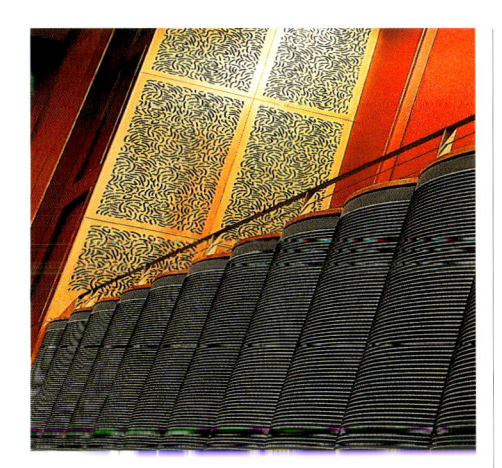

Bligh Voller Nield Pty Ltd
Sydney, Melbourne, Brisbane, Canberra; Australia

Bligh Voller Nield Pty Ltd is one of Australia's major architectural practices with experience in a wide range of building projects. This third generation practice, is noted for its innovative architecture and collaborative approach developed over 71 years. The firm comprises 11 principals; Michael Adams, Christopher Alcock, Graham Bligh, Christopher Clarke, Robert Gardner, James Grose, Neil Hanson, Lawrence Nield, Phillip Page, Phillip Tait, Shane Thompson and Jon Voller, together with nine practice directors and 13 associates and a technical and administrative staff of 135. Offices are located in Brisbane, Sydney, Canberra and Melbourne, with joint ventures in Cairns, Hong Kong, Malaysia and Papua New Guinea. Our specialist Health Group is Bligh Nield Health and in 1994 the joint venture, Bligh Lobb Sports Architecture, was established to carry out major sports projects. The practice has earned a reputation for the successful completion of major and special projects, often of a one-off nature.

Significant projects include the Australia Stadium for the Sydney 2000 Olympics, Brisbane Airport International and Domestic Terminals, World Expo '88 Brisbane, National Science and Technology Museum Canberra, 111 George Street State Government Office Tower Brisbane, Queensland Conservatorium of Music for Griffith University, Westmead Children's Hospital Sydney and the Overseas Passenger Terminal Redevelopment, Sydney.

Bligh Voller Nield is proud of the recognition given to their work through the receipt of many design awards and extensive publication of their work both nationally and internationally. More significantly, it is the pride that comes from having many satisfied clients and happy users of their buildings that provides the impetus to continue their work.

Du Bose Associates, Inc. Architects
Hartford, Connecticut, USA

For four decades, Du Bose Associates, Inc. Architects has continuously built its award-winning practice, offering architectural, planning, and interior design services, and providing thoughtful, constructive and distinctive project solutions. The firm's emphasis is on superior quality, service, diversity and identifying creative opportunities within each project. The firm specialises in educational, corporate and institutional design, with additional expertise in ADA and code-compliance issues.

The design of the landmark ECSU Library and Clock Tower is among several projects completed for ECSU including the campus master plan and the new classroom building. Other recent educational projects include two new dormitories for The Loomis Chaffee School; a major renovation of the North Dormitory Complex for Connecticut College; an addition to the University of Rhode Island's Engineering Complex; and the new Science Center of Connecticut, soon to be constructed on the banks of the Connecticut River in East Hartford.

Du Bose Associates staff is made up of seasoned, dedicated professionals who are constantly studying and staying abreast of current techniques and technologies. The staff includes experts in the latest AutoCAD, graphic and 3-D animation software packages.

The firm has offices in Hartford, Connecticut and Westerly, Rhode Island.

Earl R. Flansburgh + Associates, Inc.
Boston, Massachusetts, USA

Earl R. Flansburgh + Associates, Inc. is a Boston-based design firm providing comprehensive services in architecture, master planning, space planning, and interior design. Founded in 1963, the firm serves a broad clientele in business, industry and education in New England, throughout the United States and abroad.

For over three decades, the firm has refined a project approach that integrates a collaborative design process with the production of high quality contract documents to meet diverse clients' program requirements within budget and schedule restraints. The interface of disciplines occurs during all phases of the design process, so the result is comprehensive and unified. The approach enables the firm to provide an overall standard of excellence in both interior and exterior building design.

The long standing leadership of the firm's principals - Earl R. Flansburgh, FAIA, *President*, David S. Soleau, AIA, *Executive Vice President*, Kate M. Brannelly, *Vice President/Director of Marketing*, Alan S. Ross, AIA, *Principal*, and Duncan P. McClellan, AIA, *Principal* and the continued dedication and professionalism of a 70-person design staff, has gained the firm a national reputation for design excellence, technical skill and cost control. Recognition of their professional expertise and innovative designs have won the firm 93 national and regional design awards, and their work continues to be published in professional books and journals.

The firm has specialised in the programming, planning and design of educational facilities, including public and private primary and secondary schools, and colleges and universities.

The firm's work has encompassed over 300 projects ranging from the master plan of a new 12,000-student university campus, to the renovation and expansion of an existing law school. Some of their clients include the *Easton Public Schools, Everett Public Schools, Malden Public Schools, Thayer Academy, Lawrence Public Schools, Boston College, Worcester Polytechnic Institute, Solomon Schechter Day School* and the *University of Northern British Columbia*.

Ellenzweig Associates, Inc.
Cambridge, Massachusetts, USA

Established in 1965, Ellenzweig Associates has built a reputation for innovation in the architectural design of teaching and research facilities. With a staff of 60 operating from a single office in Cambridge, Massachusetts, the firm provides comprehensive professional design services including programming, feasibility studies, master planning, and full architectural services—schematic design, design development, construction documents, and construction administration.

Ellenzweig Associates specialises in complex, technically challenging projects—state-of-the-art teaching facilities for academic clients; research facilities for academic, biomedical, and corporate clients; and transportation-related facilities for municipal clients. Initial commissions at Harvard University and the Massachusetts Institute of Technology launched the firm's continuing focus on teaching and research facilities. Primarily serving universities and colleges, Ellenzweig Associates has planned and designed science and technology facilities, classroom buildings, libraries, art buildings, student centres, athletic facilities, and student residences. The firm's commitment to design excellence and client satisfaction is reflected in long-term relationships with many repeat clients.

Ellenzweig Associates has won over 70 design awards, including two recent Honour Awards from the American Institute of Architects (AIA) and two Honour Awards for Design Excellence from the Boston Society of Architects. Recently published projects have appeared in *Architecture*, *Architectural Record*, and *Spazio e società*.

Ellenzweig Associates, Inc.
Architects

Mitsuru Senda & Environment Design Institute
Tokyo, Japan

Mitsuru Senda is a professor of Tokyo Institute of Technology, and a honorary president of the Environment Design Institute (EDI) in Tokyo, Japan. For the past 30 years he has specialised in designing play structures and play environments for children. He has won several professional design awards and took a doctorate by a thesis "the research of the structure of children's play environment" in 1982.

He states "specialised design categories such as cities, buildings, landscape, play equipment, and interiors should not be designed separately; they must be designed totally. It is the environmental design". Based on this policy, when designing a space or area, he values the story—such as history, life, animals, and people—being there, and he introduces himself as "the environment architect". He has wrapped up his design policy into a few publications, one example being *Design of Children's Play Environments* and is planning to publish two new books *Play Space for Children* and *Play Structure*.

Mitsuru Senda established EDI in 1968 which provides city planning, regional planning, public design, architectural design, landscape design, interior design, products' design, and display design from research to design control consistency. EDI has designed parks, museums, children's centres, schools, dwellings and sports' facilities.

環境デザイン研究所

Flad & Associates
Madison, Wisconsin, USA

The Flad organisation was founded in 1927 as a family-owned architectural practice, and today ranks twenty-fifth in size in the United States. Owned and managed by its 12 working principals, Flad serves clients around the globe from regional offices across the United States. Flad's operational philosophy is to be available and close to clients, drawing on the strength of its professional staff of 250 people nationwide. Full service planning and design is provided from regional offices in Madison, Wisconsin; Gainsville, Florida; Stamford, Connecticut; San Francisco, California; Research Triangle Park, North Carolina; and St. Louis, Missouri.

Firm clients include national and international knowledge-based organisations with specialised facility needs. Discovery and innovation in work process, streamlined methods for research and production, and high performance, technology-driven environments characterise the client facilities they design.

Design specialties include R&D laboratories and process/production facilities for the pharmaceutical, biotechnology, industrial, agriculture and chemical industries; office facilities, training centres, and data centres; academic facilities; and a wide array of healthcare facilities for hospital systems, managed care networks, and university medical centres. Flad offers a full array of design services including strategic facility planning, master planning, programming, architectural design, interior architecture, landscape, graphic design, structural engineering, and construction administration.

Flad & Associates is nationally known for their planning and design presentations at national symposiums. Through focused research and seminars, the firm strives to continually be a leader in innovative design and research contributions to the profession.

FLAD

Macks and Robinson Pty Ltd
Townsville, Queensland, Australia

The firm was established in 1963 by K.J. Macks in Townsville, North Queensland. Branch offices were established in Cairns in 1965, Mackay in 1968, Ayr in 1974 and Proserpine in 1982. The company currently operates from Townsville.

Since its inception, the firm has received over 3,000 commissions throughout the whole spectrum of building sizes and types spread over the whole of North Queensland.

The company's staff have been involved in specific overseas research projects for UNESCO, AIDAB, UNDP and others in Bangladesh, Sri Lanka, Vietnam, China, Fiji, Mauritius, Reunion Island, Vanuatu, the Seychelles, Tonga, Brunei and Indonesia.

Macks and Robinson Pty Ltd has, and is building on, special expertise in cyclone resistant design and energy management, master planning, restoration and recycling of old buildings, and architectural education in addition to normal design functions.

The company sees itself as part of a team of client groups, design groups and construction groups whose responsibility is to produce well designed buildings within financial and time constraints that suit the owner, users and the community. Close attention to design for tropical conditions has, over the years, developed special skills in this field.

The company has an enviable reputation for quality documentation and contract administration.

ARCHITECTS

MacLachlan, Cornelius & Filoni, Inc.
Architecture Planning & Interior Design
Pennsylvania, USA

MacLachlan, Cornelius & Filoni, Inc. Architecture Planning & Interior Design (MCF) is a full-service architectural firm providing architectural design, master planning, programming, interior design and construction administration services. The firm has practiced architecture with a diverse clientele of educators throughout its 109 year history. MCF has provided architectural services for elementary, secondary and higher educational facilities; public, private and religious institutions; and schools for those with special needs.

Through the firms experience, they have gained a regional reputation and work with clients from North Carolina to Michigan and Illinois to Delaware. Their work respects the budget and schedule of each client and they are skilled in dealing with issues common to educational facilities: administrative goals, faculty requirements, space utilisation, and social and recreational needs. This thorough understanding of each client's aspirations coupled with their passion for building well guides MacLachlan, Cornelius & Filoni in creating enduring architecture.

MacLachlan Cornelius & Filoni
ARCHITECTURE PLANNING INTERIOR DESIGN

NBBJ
Seattle, Washington, USA

Founded in Seattle in 1943 and driven by design excellence and high standards of service, NBBJ has grown to become a national and international practice, grounded in design-focused leadership. Today, NBBJ is the third largest architectural firm in the United States—fifth largest in the world—and employs over 700 professionals in six U.S. cities: Seattle, Columbus, San Francisco, Los Angeles, New York, and Research Triangle Park (N.C.). NBBJ's wide range of services include: architecture; programming; interior design and space planning; facilities management; economics and financial feasibility; land use planning; and graphic design. The firm's markets include health care, corporate design/ interiors, sports & entertainment, airports/ transportation, commercial/mixed-use, higher education, hospitality & resorts, justice, senior housing, research and advanced technology, graphic/ environmental design, and urban design. NBBJ is currently working on projects throughout North America, Asia, Europe, and Latin America.

NBBJ

Shepheard Epstein Hunter
London, UK

Shepheard Epstein Hunter is an established practice of architects, landscape architects and planners. Many of the firm's university projects start with an overall development plan and carry through to individual buildings. Long relationships have been maintained with a number of educational institutions which have allowed the firm to assess the impact of their design decisions over a number of years, (or decades in some cases). Clients include the London School of Economics, Hull, Lancaster, and Warwick Universities, the Open University and Kings College London. Recent projects range from the conversion of Clement House from a 300-person Edwardian office building to a teaching building for 1,100 people fully equipped for computer learning for the LSE, through to new teaching and office accommodation for Hull and Warwick Universities to a new student village for Lancaster University, and smaller, complicated entrance and adaptation projects for Kings College London on the Strand.

Tai Soo Kim Partners
Hartford, Connecticut, USA

Tai Soo Kim Partners was established in 1970 in Hartford as the Hartford Design Group. In 1991, the firm was renamed to reflect the creative leadership of its founder, Tai Soo Kim, FAIA, and to recognise Mr. Kim's longtime-collaboration with Ryszard Szczypek, AIA and T. Whitcomb Iglehart, AIA. Today, the firm has a staff of 23 in its Connecticut, USA office and a 10-person affiliate office in Korea.

The firm has a diverse portfolio of projects, ranging from corporate, cultural, educational and commercial. The work is widely recognised for its unique simplicity, elegance and suitability to the natural and cultural conditions of a place.

Tai Soo Kim Partners has won a number of design awards and international design competitions including: National Museum of Contemporary Art in Korea, the Tong Yang Headquarters in Seoul, and honourable mention in the Pusan Hi-Speed Rail Station competition, also in Korea.

Among its award-winning completed projects are the Helen & Harry Gray Court for the Wadsworth Atheneum; the Corporate Training Center for the Kook Min Insurance Company of Korea; the Middlebury Elementary School in Connecticut, the Recreation Center at Miss Porter's School; the KyoBo Corporate Training Center in Korea; the United States Naval Submarine Training Facility in Groton; and, Hartford's Union Station.

Current projects include a headquarters expansion for the Daewoo Group; the Central City Development in Seoul; and, the Learning Corridor, a public/private sector urban educational campus in Hartford, Connecticut.

TAMS Consultants, Inc. Architects, Engineers and Planners
Boston, Massachusetts, USA

Established in 1942, TAMS is a collaborative design practice, drawing on the interdisciplinary talents of in-house architects, engineers and planners for projects world-wide. With offices in Connecticut, Illinois, Massachusetts, New Jersey, New York, Virginia, London, Bangkok, and Abu Dhabi, TAMS' staff of 450 have developed a reputation for excellence in the planning, design and construction of facilities for institutions, education, transportation, aviation, and infrastructure.

The projects featured in this publication were designed by TAMS' 65-person Boston Office, under the design direction of Chris Iwerks, AIA and Deborah Fennick, AIA. TAMS maintains a generalist design practice with a broad diversity of professional capabilities. The collaborative nature of their architecture, engineering and planning expertise makes TAMS appropriate for a wide range of project types where integrated site/building solutions are critical.

TAMS' design approach is responsive to the unique parameters and conditions of each project. The resulting design solutions vary widely in appearance but are related by an underlying set of core values: response to context, clarity of elements, attention to detail, spatial richness, modelling and control of natural light, and the economical use of materials and systems.

Emerging from TAMS' architectural/engineering roots, the firm's orientation has consistently focused on the expressive potential of current and emerging construction techniques. Traditional stereotomic materials (load-bearing solids with compressive strength) composed interdependently with isotropic materials (materials equally strong in all directions) form the basis of an understandable yet poetic visual language for each project.

Shepheard Epstein Hunter
London, UK

TAI SOO KIM

TAMS

The S/L/A/M Collaborative
Glastonbury, Connecticut, USA

The S/L/A/M Collaborative is a full-service architectural firm with 140 dedicated professionals, known for planning and designing institutional projects throughout the United States. The firm's areas of expertise include campus master planning, research facilities, educational facilities, healthcare environments, corporate facilities, criminal justice projects, and other complex assignments. In addition, it has inhouse interior design, structural engineering and landscape architecture studios. Staff members also teach architecture at levels ranking from secondary schools to graduate courses at Yale University.

The S/L/A/M Collaborative's projects range from small renovations and additions to large, highly technical complex buildings. Organised into design studios, the firm commits consistent team resources to a project from inception to completion to insure continuity and personalised service. It has created a synergy of team, talent and ideas, enabling them to draw from a deep pool of collective experience to meet the needs of the clients.

The staff have the expertise and experience necessary to ensure projects are completed on time, without cost overruns. The S/L/A/M Collaborative are well acquainted with regulatory agency procedures and provide facilities' planning that saves operational costs, incorporates advanced technological systems, and provides the most efficient utilisation of space. Because of the firm's ability to understand the planning and design requirements of its institutional clients, it is able to help administrators understand the unique qualities of the campus. This helps form action plans that will provide long-range direction of the facilities' programs. In addition to familiarity with technical design issues, the firm is extremely knowledgeable about the related concerns which face administrators during a building program. The firm also provides master planning services to many organisations to optimise use of existing buildings and to improve campus circulation.

Throughout the years many of The S/L/A/M Collaborative's projects have been honoured for design excellence. Recently the firm was ranked among the top design firms in the country by several publications, including *Building Design & Construction; Engineering News Records*, and *Modern Healthcare*.

The Stubbins Associates, Inc.
Cambridge, Massachusetts, USA

The Stubbins Associates, Inc. (TSA) is an architectural, planning, and interior design firm with experience in a broad range of planning solutions and building types including research facilities, libraries, office buildings, theatres and auditoriums, recreation facilities, hotels and housing as well as educational and transportation facilities. Current clients are major corporations, government agencies, developers, and colleges and universities throughout the United States and abroad. Established in 1949, the firm is currently directed by six principals and has a staff of 75 professionals. Services include feasibility studies, programming and master planning; architectural, interior and landscape design; and technical services including construction documentation and construction administration.

TSA is one of the few firms to have been awarded the prestigious "Architectural Firm Award" by the American Institute of Architects, placing it at the highest echelon of the profession. In addition, TSA's projects have won more than 150 awards for design excellence, both nationally and internationally. Some of its better known projects include Citicorp Center in New York, the Federal Reserve Bank of Boston, the Ronald Reagan Presidential Library in California, Congress Hall in Berlin and the Landmark Tower in Yokohama—the tallest building in Japan.

Tsoi/Kobus & Associates, Inc.
Cambridge, Massachusetts, USA

Tsoi/Kobus & Associates (TK&A) is the fourth largest architectural firm in the Boston Area. TK&A helps educational institutions compete for students, faculty, and supporters through the design of superior learning and research environments. Often these facilities involve new prototypes and technological innovations which support forward-looking pedagogical and research programs.

Among the most prominent academic projects underway in the northeast are two facilities by TK&A—Suffolk University Law School and Boston College Student Centre and Academic Building. The firm's clients also include Harvard Medical School, Massachusetts Institute of Technology, University of Massachusetts, University of Chicago Hospitals, and Ohio State Medical Center.

The firm's services include master planning, strategic facility planning, site evaluation, programming, feasibility assessment, architecture, interior design, building investigation, permitting support, marketing and fund-raising support, on-line project management, digital graphic representation, and project delivery strategy.

Winner of more than 30 design awards in the past decade, Tsoi/Kobus & Associates was named in 1997 by *Architectural Record* magazine as one of the country's 'best managed firms'. TK&A frequently sponsors and presents at conferences for academic administrators and faculty.

Index

A.J. Diamond, Donald Schmitt and Company	137, 138, 139, 152, 153, 172, 173, 174, 175, 180, 181
A.J. Diamond, Donald Schmitt and Company with Bregman & Hamann	118, 119
Alfred Wong Partnership Pte Ltd	17, 169
Ancher Mortlock and Woolley	186
Antoine Predock Architect FAIA	82, 83, 89, 130, 131, 132, 133
Architektenburo K. van Velsen B.V.	186, 187
Austin-Smith:Lord	14, 86, 87, 172
Barton Myers Associates Inc.	132, 133, 134, 135
Barton Myers Associates Inc./KPMB	192, 193
Blauel Architects, London	196, 197
Birgitta Holm Arkitektkontor AB	34, 35
Bligh Voller Nield Pty Ltd	84, 85
Cannon	122
Cox Richardson	100, 101, 166, 167, 168, 169, 198, 199
CZWG Architects	10, 11, 12, 13, 54, 55
Du Bose Associates, Inc., Architects	194, 195
Earl R. Flansburgh + Associates, Inc.	36, 37
Ellenzweig Associates, Inc.	112, 113, 114, 148, 149, 150, 151
Enzo Zacchiroli Architetto	106
Fentress Bradburn Architects	60, 61, 62, 63, 70, 71, 72, 73, 102, 103
Flad & Associates	120, 121
Foster and Partners	58, 59, 122, 123, 124, 125, 182, 183
Michael Graves, Architects	104, 105, 110, 111, 136, 137
Günter Domenig	38, 39
Gwathmey Siegel & Associates Architects	76, 77, 78, 79, 92, 93, 96, 97, 116, 117, 203, 204, 205, 206, 207, 208, 209, 210, 211
Hardy Holzman Pfeiffer Associates	15, 16, 17, 42, 43, 50, 51, 68, 69, 74, 75, 80, 81, 147
Margaret Helfand Architects	140, 141
Jestico + Whiles	14

Kisho Kurokawa Architect & Associates	26, 27, 28, 29
Kunchook - Moonhwa Architects & Engineers	176, 177, 178, 179
Mackey Mitchell Associates	144, 145, 146, 147, 190, 191
Macks & Robinson Pty Ltd	88
MacLachlan, Cornelius & Filoni, Inc.	154, 155
Mitsuru Senda & Environment Design Institute	8, 9
NBBJ	170, 171, 184, 185
Nelson Chen Architects	158, 159, 160, 161
Powell Dods & Thorpe	46, 47
R.M.Kliment & Frances Halsband Architects	64, 65, 66, 67, 94, 95, 97, 98, 99
Riken Yamamoto & Field Shop	40, 41
Roth and Moore Architects	20, 21
Shepheard Epstein Hunter	126, 127, 188, 189, 200, 201, 202, 203
Shin Takamatsu Architects & Associates	30, 31
The S/L/A/M Collaborative	18, 19, 24, 25
The Stubbins Associates, Inc.	90, 91, 108, 109, 128, 129, 142, 143
Tai Soo Kim Partners, Architects	48, 156, 157, 162, 163
TAMS Consultants, Inc.	22, 23, 32, 33, 44
Tsoi/Kobus & Associates Architects	44, 45, 106, 107, 114, 115
Williams & Boag Pty Ltd Architects	164, 165
WRS Architects, Inc.	52, 53

Acknowledgments

IMAGES is pleased to add "Education Spaces" to its compendium of design and architectural publications.

We wish to thank all participating firms for their valuable contribution to this publication.

Every effort has been made to trace the original source of copyright material contained in this book. The publishers would be pleased to hear from copyright holders to rectify any errors or omissions.

The information and illustrations in this publication have been prepared and supplied by the entrants. While all reasonable efforts have been made to source the required information and ensure accuracy, the publishers do not, under any circumstances, accept responsibility for errors, omissions and representations express or implied.